Social Ethics

Social Ethics

*An Examination
of American Moral Traditions*

Roger G. Betsworth

Jim:

*I hope you enjoy
reading this. I did a
lot of research in
"your" library.*

Roger

Westminster/John Knox Press
Louisville, Kentucky

Book design by Gene Harris

First edition

Published by Westminster/John Knox Press
Louisville, Kentucky

PRINTED IN THE UNITED STATES OF AMERICA
9 8 7 6 5 4 3 2 1

Library of Congress Cataloging-in-Publication Data

Betsworth, Roger G., 1933–
    Social ethics : an examination of American moral traditions
Roger G. Betsworth. — 1st ed.
        p.   cm.
    Includes bibliographical references.
    ISBN 0-664-25092-0

    1. Christian ethics—United States.   2. Social ethics.
3. Sociology, Christian—United States.   4. Church and social
problems—United States.   5. United States—Moral
conditions.
6. United States—History—Philosophy.   I. Title.
BJ1251.B47 1990
241'.096—dc20   89-29309
                                                          CIP

Always for Joan,

and also for

Mom and Dad,
who taught me the biblical story,

David and April, Deborah and Sharon,
who take up the story in their generation,

and

Christopher,
who is just beginning to learn the song

Contents

Acknowledgments

Like that of so many others who teach in small liberal arts colleges, my primary work is teaching undergraduate students. This book slowly emerged as a result of teaching social ethics to students whose intellectual and vocational interests are not in the area of religion. First, then, I wish to acknowledge the contributions of the many students who took up this way of thinking and who sought more clarity from me and for themselves.

Second, I wish to express my appreciation to my faculty colleagues, who have sustained me with an ongoing conversation about the moral traditions in American culture. Bruce Haddox, who teaches religion with me, provided a crucial impetus in the beginning of the project by spending hours helping me think through the basic direction of the study. He carefully critiqued the introduction and the conclusion. Todd Lieber, my colleague in American studies and English, has introduced me to much of the literature in American studies and was very helpful in his criticism of some of the chapters. Owen Duncan, one of our historians, helped me think about the work of Christopher Lasch and Robert Bellah. Jane Kvetko, who teaches sociology and social work, had the students in her course "Women: The Struggle for Equality" read chapter 6 and discuss it with me, and she has continued a conversation with me about feminist issues in American culture.

I also appreciate the comments and encouragement of my colleagues in the Project on Religion and American

Culture at Indiana University, Indianapolis. Shannon Jung took an early interest in the manuscript and provided supportive criticism. Rowland Sherrill and Max Stackhouse read the rough draft and suggested important revisions. In addition to these colleagues, Walter Brueggemann also read the manuscript and offered helpful suggestions.

The editorial work of John Gibbs of Westminster/John Knox Press improved the text a great deal. I appreciate all these colleagues who so willingly gave of their time. The limitations that remain are surely a result of my inability to respond to good advice.

Finally, I am immeasurably indebted to my family for their support. David, Deborah, and Sharon sustained us with their affection and humor while they engaged in conversation on these topics all through their college years. And beyond my ability to express it, I am indebted to Joan for her care, her friendship, and her love.

Social Ethics

1

Introduction

This invitation to the thought and practice of social ethics is rooted in both the plurality and the unity of the
American experience. What follows is as much a part of
the dialogue in American studies as it is an exercise in
social ethics, in knowing ourselves and guiding our actions. My perspective on so large an undertaking is shaped
by my experience in a particular community that was both
religious and American, and both of these in varied ways.
Let us begin with the issue that arose there and continues
to arise throughout American communities.

Americans have shared a distinctive American perspective even while holding widely differing understandings of
themselves and the world in which they live. The congregations I pastored during the sixties in Southern California
reflected both these differences and this common perspective.[1]

There was amazing diversity in the way people imagined
what the central concerns of Christians ought to be in
American culture in the early 1960s. Some of our people
thought civil rights was a central concern. To them, Martin
Luther King, Jr., exemplified the life of discipleship. They
argued that we, as a church, ought to take up the cause of
racial justice. They formed a core group who established a
Head Start program in the church for Mexican American
children and organized a fair housing committee in our
suburban community.

Others thought, however, that King himself was the

cause of racial troubles. They argued that America had come a long way since slavery and that "trying to go too far too fast" was inimical to racial harmony. They argued that Christians ought not to take sides in the civil rights conflict but to be mediators and seek peace.

Some young couples became convinced that the war in Vietnam ought to be a central concern for Christians. When *The Viet-Nam Reader* was published in 1967, they organized a Sunday evening Vietnam seminar.[2] As seminar participants began to study and debate the American involvement in Vietnam, two different perspectives on the relationship of America to the world emerged. Most of the participants came to believe that America ought to encourage the establishment of democracy around the world by means of example and economic aid but not by means of war.

On the other hand, others argued that the most important challenge to America was the defeat of communism. For this group, the war was part of the mission of America and ought to be supported. A large part of the congregation did not participate in the seminar but nonetheless supported both it and the draft counseling group that arose in response to it. Others bitterly denounced both groups as subverting true Christianity and patriotic American values.

Some churchwomen organized support groups for mothers of small children. As the women began to discover that their personal problems were rooted in social realities, a feminist critique of marriage began to emerge. After many hours of facilitating support groups and counseling with troubled couples I slowly came to agree with the women that there was a "his marriage" and a "her marriage" in our culture. Marriage, like other American institutions, was a relationship biased in favor of men. This cultural reality transcended the particular differences between the two persons caught up in any one marriage conflict.

Women responded in differing ways to this emerging insight. Some of them began to read and talk about Betty

Friedan's *The Feminine Mystique* in order to develop their new perspective.[3] Others opposed the emerging feminist understandings and poured more energy into meeting the needs of their husbands and children in ways that conformed to the patriarchal tradition of the culture.

Many persons did not respond to any of these concerns but thought that the primary purpose of religion was peace of mind. Peace of mind was expressed in two different languages. First, the older language of our tradition spoke of the personal peace a person gained through trust in Christ. Although earlier Methodists were inspired to care for the larger community by this tradition, in the sixties it had narrowed to a concern for the spiritual well-being of the individual. Second, not far from our church, Robert Schuller was proclaiming that true faith was faith in the power of positive thinking. For success-oriented persons in our congregations, faith in the power of positive thinking was an important addition to the classic hard-work-equals-success doctrine of the Protestant ethic. But for most persons, as for Schuller himself, positive thinking was directed toward self-esteem or peace of mind, which was an end in itself. In contrast, others in the congregation imagined that genuine Christians could have no peace of mind in the face of the plight of the poor, especially the migrant workers of California and the oppressed minorities in the ghettos of the Los Angeles area.

Yet in the face of such varied central convictions, an increasing number of young families united with our church each year in order to give their children "moral guidance in a morally confusing world." They rightfully assumed that raising their children was the most important moral task most of them would be given. They assumed, further, that the church was the sort of community in which they and the children could develop the character necessary to meet the moral challenges of our time. But with its diversity of conflicting commitments, the congregation was barely such a community.

We were forced to face the basic question of how we could become a community of common purpose and

shared vision. We began by asking a familiar ethical question: In the light of the biblical narrative, how ought we to
guide our action? But as we discovered how differently we
saw the central issues of contemporary life, we began to
raise a prior set of questions that are fundamental to social
ethics: How do we understand ourselves and the world in
which we live? How have we become the persons that we
are? Why do we see the world as we see it? Our interest in
asking these questions was the same as that of the parents
who joined the church. We wanted to live in a community
in which we and our children could develop the character
necessary to meet the moral challenges of our time.[4]

Somehow we had sensed the influence of community on
persons, and we were in quest of a more faithful community for the building of character. But we had no conceptual handle on the nature of community life and its
influence on us as moral agents. We needed to be able to
see how we were shaped by society and, in turn, how we
were the shapers of the society in which we lived. We
needed to see how our culture built a world of meaning
around us, how it informed our decisions and choices, how
it was the first interpreter to us of ourselves, and how we
could learn to mature into our interpretations and varia-
tions of self and culture. In brief, we needed to understand
how the reciprocal relationship between self and society
works.

However, any community in which we live—the family,
the church, the college, the town, the state, or the nation—
has many different understandings of self and world because American culture itself is a culture of contending
visions. Since we all must live in our culture even as we
live in our bodies, the best way to understand our moral
confusions is to examine the cultural narratives by which
our sense of self and world is shaped. Our primary interest
in such a study is to evaluate the adequacy of each narrative's moral vision. But there is also a second motive: If we
are able to find one story that can serve as a master image
for our lives, we shall be a step farther along the road of
discovering how to develop the character we seek.

Cultural Narratives

Clifford Geertz clarifies the reciprocity between self and society when he argues that we each learn what it means to be human under the guidance of cultural patterns. A cultural pattern is a "historically created system of meaning in terms of which we give form, order, point, and direction to our lives." Narrative is one of the primary ways in which a culture patterns our lives. Through narrative, cultural communities "communicate, perpetuate, and develop knowledge about and attitudes toward life." Accordingly, the narratives of a culture are not disinterested observations of experience. They organize experience into a quite definite frame of meaning and seek to teach us to think in the same way.[5]

Cultural narratives differ from ordinary stories told in a culture. In order to be told, a story must be set within a world. The cultural narrative establishes the world in which an ordinary story makes sense. It informs people's sense of the story in which they set the story of their own lives. The history, scriptures, and literary narratives of a culture, the stories told of and in family and clan, and the stories of popular culture all articulate and clarify the world of the cultural narrative in which they are set. Thus a cultural narrative is not directly told. Indeed, the culture itself seems to be telling the cultural narratives. As Geertz puts it, a culture *is* a historically transmitted pattern of meanings embodied in symbolic forms.[6]

A cultural narrative is, then, one of the basic stories that a culture is telling. We come to awareness as human beings in the midst of communities where language, metaphors, and stories already articulate, clarify, and establish our sense of self and world. Because they fashion a world, cultural narratives establish those distinctions between right and wrong actions that direct the self outward toward communal purposes in which alone the self can be realized. Our character reflects the cultural narrative that we have made our own.[7]

Geertz also suggests that within any culture the number

of cultural narratives is limited. A people can have only a few such narratives or their sense of self and world becomes so diffuse that no common pattern of meaning can emerge to give form and order to life. What has come to be defined as a culture has only a small number of world-shaping stories. In modern culture, however, the cultural narratives seldom are in full agreement with one another. A vital culture is usually a dramatic argument about the meaning of the destiny its members share, and American culture is no exception.[8]

Four dominant American cultural narratives have shaped the sense of self and world for the majority of Americans. These are: the biblical story of covenant, the Enlightenment story of progress, the story of well-being, and the story of America's mission in the world.

First, the biblical story was a principal force in the creation of American culture. The Puritans recovered the biblical understanding of covenant. They understood the human condition and judged the goodness of their actions in light of God's covenant gift: "I will be your God and you shall be my people." They sought to be faithful to Jesus' command that they love both God and neighbor, for faithfulness was the appropriate response to the gift of the covenant. As the Great Awakenings carried this point of view across America, the biblical story became established as an American cultural narrative.[9]

Second, the Enlightenment enabled Americans to develop a story of progress. Enlightenment thinkers were convinced that both the physical and moral aspects of the universe were rationally ordered, and that human beings, as creatures of reason, were able to discover that order and shape their lives to conform to it. Progress was defined as the discovery of and adherence to the laws that govern the world. Because the laws of nature were considered to be good, the person who strove to progress was considered virtuous.

However, the story of progress took on an additional economic meaning in America. In accord with the prevalent notion of virtue, it was considered moral to discover and adhere to the economic laws of the universe that enabled a person to gain financial success. Accordingly, the person who succeeded in business became the moral as well as the economic model of the emerging capitalist civilization. The story of the self-made man, or the story of success, became the best-known variant of the cultural narrative of progress. This story tells of a world in which our selves and our fortunes are shaped by our own hard work rather than by God's covenanting action.

Third, in the twentieth century, the story of well-being occupies center place as the dominant cultural narrative in America. The self is no longer described in terms of faithfulness to the covenant or in the language of hard work or duty. In the present ethos the self is spoken of in terms of achieving self-realization, self-worth, or self-esteem. Success is imagined in terms of creating an inner sense of well-being. Therapeutic images are dominant in the story of well-being, for therapeutic theory, language, and practice all serve as a resource for helping persons re-vision their lives so that they may develop a more enduring sense of well-being.

The fourth cultural narrative is the story of the mission of America. This story shapes the way Americans understand their corporate role in the world community. The mission of America arises from the conviction that, from its founding, America has been endowed with a special worldwide destiny. This special destiny is understood in two ways. First, America is an example to the nations, a proof that a free people can govern themselves in peace and justice; second, America has the responsibility to encourage and extend the freedom of all peoples.

Because the mission of America tells of a special destiny for the nation and not for the individual or the communities within the nation, it is a narrative that shapes the understanding of self when a person is acting as a member of the national community. The mission-of-America story emphasizes the corporate social reality in which our lives are set. Since this story arose early in our corporate life, it readily uses images from both the biblical story and the Enlightenment story of progress.

The biblical story, the Enlightenment story of progress, the story of well-being, and the mission of America all claim to express the truth of the human condition. For the majority of Americans, these are the perennial and most pervasive narratives that frame the ongoing cultural argument about who we are and who we ought to be.

Looking back at my experiences in the sixties, I can now see how we all make one or another of these stories a master image, to which we subordinate the other cultural narratives. Because we live in American culture, in some way we each live in all these visions of self and world. But each one of us takes up one of these stories as our primary dwelling place, and from that vantage point each of us envisions his or her central concerns.

As we make one of these stories our own and use it to give shape to our sense of self and world, then we become shapers of the world in which we live. We identify with one of the narratives of the culture and take it up as our own personal perspective. We bring our own creative powers into play as our retelling of the cultural narrative causes it to resonate with our own inimitable styles. We have become those who represent and express the culture itself; we are the ones who teach the next generation the language in which it will think. We create the families, celebrate the religion, establish the schools, and tell the stories that provide the images of self and world by which our children will know themselves and guide their action.[10]

Insiders and Outsiders

Two questions arise at this point: (1) Why are these four cultural narratives the ones that so powerfully shape the American sense of self and world? (2) Do these narratives function in the same way among those who live inside and those who live outside the dominant groups?

To answer the first question, these cultural narratives

became powerful because they were grounded in at least three circumstances. To begin with, these were the stories in which the founders of American culture lived and with which they thought about self and world. The Puritans of New England were the leaders of church, state, and commerce. They told the biblical story from the perspective of the ruling class. Following the revolution, the story of the mission of America was the primary way the leadership interpreted the country's meaning, both to American citizens and to the world. As the center of power shifted to the emerging commercial and industrial sector, the Enlightenment story of progress was told by persons of power such as Benjamin Franklin and Andrew Carnegie. They also told the story of the mission of America in Enlightenment language. In the twentieth century, the story of well-being has been widely promulgated by those who have access to the most modern of powers, the contemporary mass media. The power to disseminate world-shaping stories has continued to be the privilege of the powerful, who have shaped the culture according to their own vision.

Second, these cultural narratives seem legitimate to the majority because the stories support a social order that already seems right. Peter Berger notes that when persons are born into a particular social order, that order legitimates itself first of all just by being there. We identify ourselves with our own families, clans, communities, and social institutions. We affirm that the way we do things is the good and true way. The cultural narratives both celebrate the goodness of our way and enable us to provide an answer when children and newcomers ask, Why? Therefore, once a story gives shape to the institutions of a culture, an ongoing process is set in motion that reconstructs and maintains that particular understanding of self and world.[11]

The third reason for these world-shaping stories to continue is that they are in some way commensurate with the experience and imagination of the majority of Americans. Although the powerful have the privilege of promulgating stories in a way that the less powerful do not, there are limits to the sort of story even they can tell. The stories must have the power to order the everyday world of most people, to give a sense of structure, purpose, and meaning to life. Such power must be inherent in the stories themselves. Cultural narratives that are too thin, too transparently self-deceptive, cannot be imposed by even the powerful upon a majority whose experience and sense of the whole is radically at odds with those who seek to control a culture.

As for the second question, these four stories, which peculiarly belong to the dominant groups, seem to the outsiders to be transparently deceptive either in themselves or in the way in which the powerful appropriate them. In America, much of the opposition to the unjust ways in which the powerful use the dominant narratives of the culture arises from the oppressed. The racism and sexism of the majority of Americans continues to deny justice, equality, and freedom to Americans of minority races and to women. Such persons and groups are thereby placed outside the promises of full participation in American society.

The reality of oppression confronts us as we take up this second question and begin to examine how these four cultural narratives function among those who live outside the dominant groups. Because many persons of minority groups both take up some of the basic themes of the major cultural stories and reject others, they are at the same time both outsiders and insiders to the American cultural narratives. W. E. B. Du Bois referred to this sense of being an outsider-insider in terms of having a "double consciousness." Black Americans, Du Bois argued, always have a dual awareness of self. On the one hand, the image of self is that of being an American. But the American sense of self includes racism, which oppresses blacks. So on the other hand, blacks also have an image of self that is rooted in the reality of being part of the black community, which opposes racism. Because blacks are always aware of being both American and black, they are able to see more clearly the ways in which the cultural narratives are used to justify racism.[12]

Because the outsiders see how the cultural narratives of the majority support an oppressive, unjust social order, outsiders seek to refashion the cultural stories by drawing on their own stories, which they have created out of their religious, historical, and cultural experiences. By turning to their own history to show how each cultural narrative has been used to justify oppression, they reorder the cultural vision of the majority. This reordering of the cultural narratives invites all Americans to envision a nation in which freedom and justice for all can be more nearly realized.

The very need for such a reordering highlights our difficulty in fully understanding ourselves. Even if we are aware of the story that is the interpretative framework in which we live, we may not notice the way we shape it to our own interests. We use the resources available in our cultural narratives to affirm rather than to critique our own life stories. But outsiders in American society, who live in the double consciousness of being American and being oppressed, are sensitive to the fact that the majority uses its story to its own advantage. Such sensitivity makes the contribution of minorities invaluable for the task of understanding ourselves and guiding our actions.

The Nature of Self-deception

Our way of imagining ourselves is so powerfully shaped by cultural narratives because the story form of thinking is a fundamental form of thought. In telling ourselves and others the story of why we are pursuing a particular course of action, we weave a story or scenario that gathers events into a whole. We fashion a continuous story out of the experienced past into the willed future. As we do this, we incarnate in story form both our experience and our sense of personal identity. On the one hand, we create the story out of our experiences. On the other hand, our experiences make sense only as they appear in the story. But since we fashion our own stories, they often reflect a more favorable view of ourselves than the experience itself might suggest. In a word, we often fashion a story of self-deception.[13]

Stories of self-deception are common because they are not difficult to create, and they enable us to avoid unpalatable truths about ourselves and our actions. As I weave into story the experiences of my life, I present myself as the character who lives in the story I am narrating. I can, however, without falsifying the events or the facts, tell the story in quite different ways. I can tell the story of my action in a way that is flattering or unflattering. If by poor judgment I make an unwise purchase of a used car, I can present myself as a victim because I am a "person who trusts other persons" or I can see myself as "gullible and naïve." If I fail to tell the whole truth and thereby mislead another person, I can tell my story in the form of confession and genuinely repent of my sin, or I can tell the story in the form of a regret and take comfort in the fact that I did the best I could under difficult circumstances. In self-deception, we have at least two stories going on at the same time.

Stephen Crites suggests that the first story going on in self-deception is the "real" story. It is fashioned by our underlying sense of how the events in which we are involved connect. This course of events includes our motives as well as our actions. The real story is so painful that we seek to deny it, yet it continues to assert itself as our basic way of interpreting our situation.

The second story is what Crites calls the "cover" story. The cover story is another way of interpreting our action; it is a way that is less painful, more honorable, and also plausible. The cover story is "cover" because it must be steadily rehearsed to self and others in order to maintain its primacy and suppress the real story. The cover story may be a story that deals with a course of action already taken. It may also be a story that enables us to avoid spelling out some aspect of our relationship to the world even in the face of a situation that seems to demand that we make explicit what we are doing.[14]

There are possibilities of self-deception other than the

real story of shame and the cover story of honor or avoidance. Sometimes the real story seems too positive or too good to be true. So the cover story is a story of irony or cynicism or rationalism, which serves to keep at a distance the reality that life often seems to be a response to gifts, or to providence, and therefore to a giver or a provider. Sometimes the cover story is the only story. A person may avow that he or she is engaged in a project when there is nothing genuinely envisioned, no commitment to discovery or to a cause. In this case the cover story conceals the fact that there is no story.

Finally, of course, each of the stories we fashion is a story shaped by the cultural narrative in which we live. Whether we are able to discern our own self-deceptions depends on the resources available to us. No cultural narrative enables its participants to avoid self-deception completely. To be is to be self-deceived. However, some cultural narratives provide accounts of how persons take up cover stories and how, with the aid of someone in their community who speaks the truth, they discover ways to return to the real story. As we have noted, persons of minority groups readily perceive the ways in which the cultural narratives are used to justify oppression. When minorities in the community exercise their vocation to speak the truth, then the whole community has the opportunity to gain the experience and the skill required to recognize self-deception and to be more faithful to the truth more of the time. Whether the majority community will respond to the truth tellers depends on the adequacy of the dominant cultural narrative. Cultural narratives that deal more heuristically with self-deception provide more adequate images of self and world.[15]

Conclusion

The biblical story, the Enlightenment story of progress, the story of well-being, and the mission of America all claim to interpret the truth of the human condition. We who live in the United States of America are shaped by the way these stories have been told in our culture. Although many of us have used each of them from time to time, most of us have used one story as our dominant figure for interpreting self and world. Therefore, in order to see more clearly what images of self and world appear in each narrative, we need to develop our understanding of the basic themes of each story. We can then see how we Americans carry on the dramatic argument about the meaning of the destiny we share. By so doing, perhaps we can discover the sort of community we need if we and our children are to develop the character necessary to meet the moral challenges of our time.

2

The Biblical Story

The biblical narrative, especially as interpreted by the Puritans' emphasis on covenant, was a major force in the creation of American culture. The Puritans thought of human history as the arena in which God gathered the saints, saving them from the fate that all deserved and imparting to them some knowledge of God's will. God's will was expressed in the biblical language of covenant.

The idea of mutual obligation, of two parties bound and committed by the terms of an agreement, was fundamental to the understanding of covenant. For the Puritans, God had freely chosen to enter into covenants with his people, even though they, because of their sin, did not deserve his promises. Since it was a free gift of God, the covenant was a covenant of grace. According to Puritan faith, the God who offered the covenant relationship to Abraham spoke his words also to them: "I will be your God, you shall be my people." To be "God's people" meant to respond to God's loving gift of the covenant by loving God and loving neighbor.[1]

The Puritan Perspective

The whole train of historical events that led to the establishment of the Massachusetts Bay Colony in Salem in 1630 was, in the understanding of the Puritans, a result of God's covenanting action. In his famous sermon on board the *Arbella* before landing, John Winthrop developed the

themes of covenant. He argued that because God had
shepherded the colonists through all the dangers of the
North Atlantic crossing and had brought them in peace to
the new land, God had offered the covenant anew to them.
New England was to be a New Israel—a covenanted community. Covenant meant that the colonists were required
to respond to God in a very specific way:

> We must entertain each other in brotherly affection; we must
> be willing to abridge ourselves of our superfluities for the
> supply of others' necessities; . . . We must delight in each
> other, make others' conditions our own, rejoice together,
> mourn together, labor and suffer together. . . . So shall we
> keep the unity of the spirit in the bond of peace, the Lord
> will be our God and delight to dwell among us, as His own
> people, and will command a blessing upon us in all our
> ways.[2]

There is a tension within this ideal of a community prac-
ticing love of God and neighbor: each individual is to obey
God first and yet at the same time submit to the will of the
group for the common good. Covenant vision seeks to accommodate the tension in two ways. First, it insists that
God calls each person to his or her place in the community. Faithfulness to one's calling in each order of creation
(family, church, workplace, school, and state) is the primary mode of expressing one's love toward God and
neighbor. This means that one's work must serve both
God and community.

Second, the conviction that "we must be willing to
abridge ourselves . . . for the supply of others" is clearly
an ideal of voluntary self-sacrifice for the common good.
The logic of the covenant is two-dimensional: When God
covenants with a people to be their God, the people are
bound to God, but the people are also bound to one another through God. If the people faithfully care and even
sacrifice for one another, they will be an example to all
peoples, a "city set on the hill," and God will bless and
prosper their community. If they do not care for one another in such a way, then the "Lord will surely break out

in wrath against us, and be revenged of such a perjured people."

Winthrop concluded his sermon with the Deuteronomic exhortation of Moses to the people of Israel as they were about to enter the Promised Land:

> Beloved, there is now set before us life and good, death and evil, in that we are commanded this day to love the Lord our God, and to love one another . . . that the Lord our God may bless us in the land whither we go to possess it: but if our hearts shall turn away so that we will not obey, but shall be seduced and worship . . . our pleasures and profits, . . . we shall surely perish out of the good land.[3]

Between 1630 and 1643, more than twenty thousand Puritans made their way from England to New England. The Puritanism from which Winthrop and the Massachusetts Bay Colony drew their vision of self and world was a widespread movement of cultural revitalization. Such movements, or Great Awakenings, arose in times of social crisis. They sought to overcome the disjunctions between old beliefs and new realities, between accepted patterns of action and new experiences. Awakenings altered the worldview of a whole people and generated a set of shared beliefs and practices. Winthrop and his cofounders of New England were full and conscious participants in the Puritan awakening in England and America that extended from about 1610 to 1640.

After the Puritan dominance subsided, especially under the impact of later immigrants who arrived with different traditions, the biblical story continued to influence the formation of American culture. The two Great Awakenings, especially, carried the power of biblical narrative into the wider culture. The first Great Awakening, extending from about 1730 to 1760, was both a great national revival and a major cultural event. It began among the Puritans, because Puritanism was, by expressed intention, a vast and extended revival movement. A new expectancy entered the life of the American people. A national sense of religious and moral resolution was born. The second Great Awakening, from about 1800 to 1830, deepened and intensified both effects. Biblical story provided the central resource for these awakenings. Thus for two centuries, from the days of the Puritan founders to the mid-nineteenth century, one of the dominant American images of self and world was drawn from the biblical narrative.[4]

The Deuteronomic Vision of Covenant

In order for us to understand more fully the Puritan world, we need to examine the Deuteronomic vision of covenant that became the master image of the Puritan self and world. As Walter Brueggemann suggests, the frame of reference for the entire biblical story is provided by the Deuteronomic interpretation of Yahweh's gift of the covenant and the community's response to that gift. Brueggemann organizes his study of the gift and the response around the three histories of the land: (1) the history of the covenant promise on the way to the land, (2) the response to the covenant in the history of the management of the land on the way into exile, and (3) the new history of covenant promise, which begins in exile and culminates in the kingdom of God.[5]

According to Brueggemann, land is a central motif in the biblical narrative. The creation story tells of Adam and Eve, who are given the gift of land: the garden of Eden. The gift of the garden also includes the gift of limits. Adam and Eve are not to eat of the tree of the knowledge of good and evil, "for in the day that you eat of it," Yahweh says, "you shall die" (Gen. 2:17). They do eat. They do not die. Instead, Yahweh casts them out of the good land to wander where the soil is cursed, yielding brambles and thistles. Brambles and thistles are indeed characteristic of the lives of Cain and all those who live before the flood.

Israel first appears in the call to Abraham to leave his country, his family, and his father's house for the land that will be given him. Israel is embodied in this story of Abraham, Isaac, and Jacob. Israel is a landless people on its way to the Promised Land. Again and again the fulfillment of the promise seems impossible, beyond belief, beyond even the reach of Yahweh. Yet Isaac and Jacob are strangely protected, and the promise is renewed with the births of Benjamin and Joseph. The story of Joseph is the story of the first settlement of Israel in the land. It is not the land of promise, but the land of Egypt. Treachery and famine carry Joseph and his brothers to Egypt. In their dramatic meeting in Egypt, Joseph tells his brothers, "Do not grieve, do not reproach yourselves for having sold me here, since God sent me before you to preserve your lives. . . . Hurry and bring my father down here" (Gen. 45:5, 13). Reconciliation thus brings the whole of Israel to settle in Egypt. But Egypt is not the promised land; it is not the land of gift; it is Pharaoh's land. Jacob and Joseph die there, still longing for the promise.

When a pharaoh arises in Egypt who knows nothing of Joseph, Israel is enslaved. The bitterness of slavery nearly crushes the hope of the promise. In the call of Moses the promise is renewed. Yahweh will bring his people up out of the land of slavery to a land rich and broad, where milk and honey flow. The plagues culminate in the Passover. Israel flees Egypt. The sea is crossed. Pharaoh is overthrown in the waters. The covenant is given anew at Mount Sinai. The heady experience of liberation from bondage fills Israel with the expectation of an immediate possession of a land of milk and honey. It is a false hope.

The gift that follows freedom is the gift of wilderness, of forty years of wanderings. Israel's response is murmuring and rebellion. In the wilderness, Israel looks in disappoint- ment back to Egypt, not forward to the Promised Land as she did in the time of the Patriarchs. Yet Yahweh is in the wilderness, giving gifts of manna, quail, and water. The gifts cannot be possessed; they cannot be owned; Israel cannot settle down and be at home in these gifts. There is just barely enough for one day. Yet in the desert of death, in the presence of her enemies, Yahweh gives life to Israel, and at last her cup runs over. Israel stands on the bank of the Jordan, looking across to the Promised Land.

It is at this point, according to Deuteronomy, that Israel

pauses and listens to Moses rehearse the gift and demand of the covenant. The new situation of land possession requires a new response of faith. Brueggemann suggests that Moses sees the land as gift and temptation, as task and threat. Therefore, Israel's response in the land may bring forth blessing or curse.

The land is gift, a gift given through the terror of war, for Yahweh intends to use Israel to punish the sins of the present inhabitants of the land. Moses reminds Israel, "It is not for any goodness or sincerity of yours that you are entering the land to possess it; no, it is for the wickedness of these nations that Yahweh your God is dispossessing them for you" (Deut. 9:5). The Israelites are being given cities not of their building, wells they did not dig, vineyards and olives they did not plant because Yahweh chose Abraham and promised him this gift. The land given is a prosperous land, where Israel will want nothing. It is not a land like the land of Egypt that must be managed, watered, and dominated in order to yield the necessities of life. No, the land given is a land that drinks water by the rain of heaven, a land Yahweh cares for. The land is therefore covenanted land. The relationship to the land must not be divorced from the relationship to Yahweh, lest the Israelites, in their turn, be driven out.

The land becomes a source of temptation when it is owned. Owners such as the pharaohs control, manage, use up, dominate, and exploit the land and the landless. In the new land, those among whom the Israelites live worship Baal, whose rites celebrate an unending cycle of production and consumption. The command "You shall not covet" makes no sense at all in the world of Baal. To own land is to have the ability to revel in one's power of production and consumption.

The sense of land as gift reverses the notion of ownership. No Israelite is to say, "This land is my own." The land is always the land that Yahweh has given, and therefore it is always covenant land. For this reason Moses warns Israel against divorcing the land from Yahweh by saying, "My own strength and the might of my own hand won this wealth for me." Such a boast rewrites history, substitutes self-ownership for gift and covetousness for covenant. Only the true history will enable Israel to resist self-deception. Therefore, at harvest time, when the land is heavy with gifts, Israel must go before Yahweh and proclaim:

> My father was a wandering Aramaean. He went down into Egypt to find refuge there, few in numbers; but there he became a nation, great, mighty, and strong. The Egyptians illtreated us, they gave us no peace and inflicted harsh slavery on us. But we called on Yahweh the God of our fathers. Yahweh heard our voice and saw our misery, our toil and our oppression; and Yahweh brought us out of Egypt with mighty hand and outstretched arm, with great terror, and with signs and wonders. He brought us here and gave us this land, a land where milk and honey flow.
>
> Deuteronomy 26:5–10

To guard against temptation, Torah is linked to the land. Torah is covenant keeping; it is the way Israel is to live within and celebrate the gift. The first task of Torah is to have no other gods. Israel is not to be self-deceived, to imagine that other gods, or the labor of their own hands, have either given them the land or will prosper them in it. Instead of ownership, there is stewardship. Yahweh is the owner of the land; Israel is to be the faithful covenant-keeping steward of Yahweh's land.

The second task of Torah is to keep the sabbath. The seventh day is a day of rest. It interrupts the unending cycle of labor on the land. Even the servants are to rest. It is a day of remembrance: "Remember that you were a servant in the land of Egypt, and that Yahweh your God brought you out from there with mighty hand and outstretched arm; because of this, Yahweh your God has commanded you to keep the sabbath day (Deut. 5:15).

The seventh year is the sabbath year. It interrupts the ordinary cycle of covetous acquisitive ownership. In the seventh year, debts are canceled and slaves are to be set free. The slave is not to go empty-handed but is to be provided for, even as Yahweh has provided for Israel (Deut.

15:1–11). Even the land itself must be rested in the seventh year. Finally, at the end of a week of years, in the seventh month, a jubilee is to be proclaimed. The jubilee is a "liberation for all the inhabitants of the land." Each person is to return to his or her ancestral home. All land is to return to the clan to which it was given by Yahweh upon Israel's entrance into the promised land.

The sabbaths of rest, debt cancellation, and slave emancipation move against the temptation to envision life as a matter of ownership, hard work, good management, and deserved success. The vision of ownership legitimates the using up of other persons, the land, and even self in the pursuit of the goal of prosperity. No workers are to be rested, no debts canceled, no slaves set free in a world ruled by owners. Owners intend to produce as much prosperity as possible in order to consume whatever one's eye covets. But sabbath keeping sustains the vision of stewardship, restrains covetousness, and releases persons from bondage to the cycle of producing and consuming.

The vision of ownership, of the right to use the land as the owner pleases, is so powerful that the third task of Torah, love for neighbor, is also marshaled against it. Those who have no land or wealth or power are to be cared for as full participants in the covenant. The poor, the stranger, the wayfarer, the widow and orphan, and the Levite are all to be treated as brothers and sisters. They must be given a share of the fruits of the covenant land. When the landed ones give to the poor, they are to give with an open heart. Workers are not to be exploited. Strangers, orphans, and widows must be dealt with justly and allowed to glean the fields behind the first pickers. Israelites are not to be owners who harden their hearts and pick their own fields a second time. This caring for one's neighbor is what it means to live in the covenant:

> And now, Israel, what does Yahweh your God ask of you? Only this: to fear Yahweh your God, to follow all his ways, to love him, to serve Yahweh your God with all your heart and all your soul. . . . Circumcise your heart then and be obsti-

nate no longer; for Yahweh your God is God of gods and Lord of lords, the great God, triumphant and terrible, never partial, never to be bribed. It is he who sees justice done for the orphan and the widow, who loves the stranger and gives him food and clothing. Love the stranger then, for you were strangers in the land of Egypt.

Deuteronomy 10:12–19

Because the land is covenant gift and Torah task, Moses sees clearly that the land is also threat. As soon as Israel forgets that the land is gift and affirms the sacredness of property rights, Israel forsakes the covenant. Or even when the community at large is faithful and encourages each person to walk in the covenant, still the individual must take up this way of seeing the world, must live in it, and must make it her or his own. When the Israelite does not take up the gift and task of Torah, then that person no longer dwells in the covenant.

Deuteronomy, therefore, sets the two ways before Israel very simply. To obey Yahweh, to accept the land as a covenant gift, to take up the task of Torah, is to choose life and blessing. To succumb to the power of temptation, to live in the vision of ownership, to forget Yahweh, to forget sabbath, to be consumed by the passion for prosperity, is to choose death and cursing. For Deuteronomy, the formula of blessings or curses applies to both the individual and the community.

The perspective of Deuteronomy is a pervasive theme in the whole of the biblical story. Israel moves from the history of covenant promise into the land, from the history of faithless ownership of the land into exile, and in exile a new history of covenant promise begins that culminates in the story of the kingdom of God. The image of the two ways resonates throughout. Faithful, full-hearted obedience secures blessings. The psalmist celebrates what he has seen:

> Yahweh takes care of good men's lives,
> and their heritage will last for ever;
> they will not be at a loss when bad times come,

in time of famine they will have more than they need.
. . . . ๏ . . . .
Now I am old, but ever since my youth
I never saw a virtuous man deserted,
or his descendants forced to beg their bread.

Psalm 37:18–19, 25

Likewise, to yield to the temptations of ownership, to divorce land from Yahweh and Torah, brings curses. The greatest of the kings, King David, neglects Torah keeping and acts as though he owns throne and land. He sees Bathsheba, desires her, takes her, arranges the death of her husband, Uriah, and marries her. For this, Nathan confronts David with the curse of Yahweh: Yahweh intends to stir up evil for David out of his own house, to take his wives and give them to his neighbors, and to strike down the child so it dies. David repents, at least, and confesses his sin to Nathan. Most of the other kings neither repent nor confess. The people follow in the way of the kings rather than in the way of the Torah. Amos speaks in tones that all the prophets echo:

Listen to this, you who trample on the needy
and try to suppress the poor people of the country,
you who . . . by lowering the bushel, raising the shekel,
by swindling and tampering with the scales . . .
buy up the poor for money,
and the needy for a pair of sandals. . . .
Yahweh swears it by the pride of Jacob,
"Never will I forget a single thing you have done.
. . . .
I am going to turn your feasts into funerals,
all your singing into lamentation;
I will have your loins all in sackcloth,
your heads all shaved."

Amos 8:4–7, 10

Not only does Israel forget covenant obligations to brothers and sisters, she also neglects to celebrate jubilee. The only celebration of jubilee, which takes place in Jeremiah's time, ends shamefully, for after the threat to Jerusalem has passed, the freedmen are reenslaved. All the prophets agree with Amos that Israel is punished and at last is sent into exile because of its faithlessness. To the gift of the covenant Promised Land, Israel responds with a management style characteristic of Egypt. It is a response that carries Israel into exile.

In the midst of the experience of exile, Israel hears again the promise of the covenant. The restatement of the covenant by Jeremiah and Ezekiel is Yahweh's new action. It is not dependent upon Israel's repentance. It is a genuinely new initiative. The response to that initiative was not new, however. It was a recovery of the Deuteronomic perspective: Faithfulness will bring blessings; faithlessness will bring punishment. When Israel returned from exile, the leadership was deeply committed to the maintenance of the Deuteronomic code as the way to survive in history.

Self-deception and the Formula of the Two Ways

From a historical perspective, however, it has become clear that the Deuteronomic code could be used either to encourage covenant faithfulness or to deepen self-deception. Israel, Yahweh, and the world their action created seemed, from the Deuteronomic point of view, to be fairly predictable—in fact, all too predictable. That point of view often was reduced to the simplistic formula of two ways: Faithfulness brings blessing; sin brings disaster. Worse yet, the formula could be reversed to say: Those who are blessed have been righteous; those who suffer disaster have been sinful.

But the central character of the biblical story does not act in so predictable a manner. Yahweh surprises us, steps outside the formula, and begins anew. Adam and Eve eat of the forbidden tree, but Yahweh has a change of mind. Instead of death, they are exiled from the garden. Yahweh's covenant with Abraham is a surprise move. Jacob surely deserves to be cursed for all his treacheries, but Yahweh wrestles with him and blesses him. Esau, who has every reason to attack Jacob, forgives him. Yahweh turns the sin of Joseph's brothers into a blessing instead of a curse.

When he becomes the powerful one, Joseph unpredictably forgives his brothers.

In the words of Amos, Yahweh promises wicked Israel a day of darkness—a day when one escapes from a lion only to meet a bear, a day that will be all gloom, without a single ray of light. But Hosea hears Yahweh reconsider that promise. Yahweh is God, not human being, and does not wish to destroy. Yahweh does punish, to be sure. Israel does go into exile. But Yahweh decides to begin again, to bring Israel back. The psalmist is convinced that Yahweh acts out of steadfast love, never punishing the people as their guilt and sin deserve. Punishment, like blessing, is therefore genuine action, a fresh beginning. Neither punishment nor blessing is a mechanical reaction required by formula. All Yahweh's deeds are paradigms of grace: they are new initiatives.

Within the biblical narrative, then, the Deuteronomic perspective is both a valuable and an inadequate way of attempting to figure the world. It is valuable for three reasons: (1) It militantly opposes all attempts to justify action in terms of narrow self-interest. It requires that action intend the good of the whole community in covenant with Yahweh. (2) It provides a sense of order in a disordered world. There is a reason for the good gifts or the chaos of evil that attends our lives. (3) The way in which Deuteronomy recasts the story also establishes Yahweh as a dependable character. His love is sure. His wrath is certain.[6]

On the other hand, the Deuteronomic perspective is inadequate to the extent that its formulaic structure lulls the prosperous into self-deception. It is easy to ignore the real story—that Yahweh gives freely—and to try to live in a cover story that tells us we are prosperous because of our righteousness but our neighbors are poor because of their sin.

Stories such as Ruth, Jonah, and Job therefore begin to appear in the biblical tradition. They spell out the self-deceptions in that cover story and provide resources to counter them. These stories stress that life consists in giving and responding to gifts. Even the meaning of gift is not singular, for tragedy may be included in the gifts given. So Naomi is given bitterness, but Ruth, the foreign woman, comes with the bitterness and turns it into blessing. Jonah refuses to go to Nineveh to denounce their sin, precisely because he rejoices in the prospect of the coming destruction of Nineveh. When Yahweh rescues Nineveh by means of Jonah himself, the Ninevites rejoice in the way of Yahweh, but Jonah, the righteous prophet of God, is angry enough to die.

Job loses family, wealth, and health. His three "friends" urge him to confess his sin, for they are convinced that good men do not suffer. "If God had a mind to speak," they tell Job, "you would know it is for sin he calls you to account" (Job 11:6). Job argues that there is no such calculus. "Innocent and guilty, he destroys all alike. When a sudden deadly scourge descends, he laughs at the plight of the innocent" (9:23). But Yahweh angrily upbraids Job and lays bare the radical limits of his understanding. No one is able to grasp the secrets of life and death, prosperity and disaster, blessing and curse. Job's tone is an echo of Jeremiah's, who accuses Yahweh of being a trickster, of being like a desert stream that fails in time of need.

Deutero-Isaiah's vision reaches beyond both Job and Jeremiah. His Servant Songs tell the story of Yahweh's servant, whose suffering is not caused by his own sin, but who is willing to suffer in order that the sins of many will be healed. He will bring good news to the poor, proclaim liberty to the enslaved, and ring in the year of jubilee.

These stories of Ruth, Jonah, Job, and the Servant subvert the established world of the Deuteronomic cover story. The way of seeing the world from within the cover story is reversed. As these narratives bring to light the ways in which Deuteronomy has been misused in the service of self-deception, they emphasize that genuine Torah keeping, which means love of God and love of neighbor, is still crucial. These stories call those who dwell in the biblical story to step back from their own engagements with the world and examine them in the light of Torah.

Covenant Promise in the Gospel According to Luke

The development of covenant promise that began in the exile continues in the New Testament as it remembers the old covenant promise. Deuteronomy is one of the most quoted books in the New Testament. When the scribe asks Jesus which is the first of all the commandments, Jesus quotes Deuteronomy:

> *Listen, Israel, the Lord our God is the one Lord, and you must love the Lord your God with all your heart, with all your soul,* with all your mind and *with all your strength.* The second is this: *You must love your neighbor as yourself.*
>
> Mark 12:29–31

Though the second law came not from Deuteronomy but from Leviticus, by Jesus' time it was an accepted summary of what the Torah required in relation to others. Since the central theme of Jesus' message was the proclamation of the kingdom of God, his willingness to restate the demands of the kingdom in the language of the Torah underlined the way the old promises were continued in the new.

Perhaps the best way to understand the character of the new covenant promise of the kingdom is to trace the life of Jesus through one of the Gospels. The Gospel that corresponds most closely to the form of biography is the Gospel according to Luke. It corresponds, of course, not to modern biographies but to the genre of Greco-Roman biographies of the period. The purpose of such a biography was to teach the reader how to imitate the hero's way of life. Luke portrays Jesus as the model to which disciples are to conform their lives.[7]

Luke divides his story into four sections. The opening section serves to set the stage for the action of Jesus. The second section tells the story of the ministry in Galilee and the call of the disciples. The third section is a long teaching section structured around the journey to Jerusalem. The fourth section deals with the final days in Jerusalem. Through this four-step story Luke leads his readers into the dynamic interactions between Jesus, the kingdom of God, the disciples, the needy, and the opponents.

The Gospel opens with stories of advent and reversal. The stories of advent display the character of the action through which God rules. The stories of reversal emphasize that the action of God directly opposes the ordinary understandings of what is good or expected within the culture. The coming of the kingdom is announced by the visitation of the angel to Zechariah and Mary and, in due time, by the visitation of many angels to the shepherds. The angels are the narrative figures who indicate that God is beginning something new. The kingdom of God is upon us; its advent is at hand.

From the beginning of the story, the kingdom that God is inaugurating reverses the ordinary expectations of the culture. Zechariah, the priest, a holy man who would be expected to hear and believe the word of the angel, is disbelieving. Mary, a simple peasant woman who would not be expected to be a messenger of God precisely because she is a woman, hears and believes. Mary deepens the reversal in the song she sings:

> *He has pulled down princes* from their thrones *and
> exalted the lowly.*
> *The hungry he has filled with good things,* the rich sent
> empty away.
>
> Luke 1:52–53

When John the Baptist comes of age, he also opposes the standards of his culture. In his sermon he proclaims that God requires a new, genuine righteousness. At the close of the sermon Jesus appears, is baptized, and while in prayer receives his commission to take up his ministry. The commissioning takes the form of the gift of the Spirit and the voice from heaven, which proclaims, "You are my son, the Beloved; my favour rests on you" (Luke 3:22).

The temptation story closes this section. The temptations invite Jesus to use his gifts to dominate and to exploit as those who have great power usually do. Jesus responds to each temptation with a quote from Deuteronomy. He makes it clear that he does not own his gifts; he cannot use them as he pleases, for they are covenant gifts given in light of his commission.

Luke sketches the characteristics of Jesus' world in these opening stories. The kingdom of God is breaking into and reversing the social and political structures. The high are being brought low, the low are being lifted up, the hungry are being filled, and the rich are being sent empty away.

Luke's story of the ministry of Jesus opens in the synagogue of Jesus' hometown. Jesus reads a text from Isaiah, which proclaims that the gift of the spirit is for the sake of the poor, the captives, the blind, and the downtrodden. The good news is this: It is the year of the Lord's favor: that is, the year of jubilee. Jubilee is a year of liberation for all inhabitants of the land. Debts are to be canceled, slaves are to be set free, land is to be returned to its original covenantal partners, and the hearts of all are to be open to the poor. The sermon is a summary of the meaning of Jesus' ministry.

At first the congregation is pleased with the sermon. But the mood soon turns ugly. Jesus promises no day of vengeance for all the wrongs Israel has suffered (Isa. 61:5) but argues instead that as both Elijah and Elisha ministered to the hungry outside of Israel so also the year of jubilee will liberate the enslaved everywhere. This widening of the year of the Lord's favor enrages the people of Jesus' hometown and sets them against him.[8]

The sermon reverses the common ways of accounting success and failure, good and evil. The good news for the poor, if it is truly the good news of the jubilee year, is bad news indeed for the rich. Certainly those who are profiting politically and economically from the present order will oppose such a program and such a prophet. In addition, those who rely on the Deuteronomic formula that the righteous will be blessed and the unrighteous cursed will oppose the heresy that Gentiles, who do not keep the law at all, will be recipients of the year of the Lord's favor. It is no surprise that the whole established order—economic, political, and religious—will soon align itself against the proclaimer of such a message.

The year of jubilee is proclaimed not only in Jesus' preaching but also in his ministry of healing. Those who are enslaved by sickness or fettered by madness are freed from their bondage. He restores social outcasts to community and forgives sinners. He heals on the sabbath, for the sabbath is a day to celebrate release from bondage. The image of the year of jubilee therefore lends meaning to the phrase *the kingdom of God.* The kingdom or reign of God is the way God acts as God rules. Jesus emphasizes that the way God is acting is to liberate the people of God from all that enslaves them: debt, prison, servanthood, inferior status, sin, sickness, madness, and landlessness. His ministry attracts large crowds and bitter opposition. Jesus responds to the crowds by withdrawing to pray and returning to minister. He responds to the opposition by selecting the twelve apostles, thus establishing an organized movement to expand and continue the work he is beginning. To the apostles, to the larger group of disciples, and to the great crowd he then preaches the "Sermon on the Plain."

In the sermon Jesus deepens his disciples' understanding of the reign of God and of the jubilee proclamation. The forgiveness of debts, the liberation of slaves, and the return of ancestral lands might well be done grudgingly, and can only be done by those who possess debts, slaves, and land. But Jesus applies the jubilee to the poor as well as the rich. The primary understanding of jubilee is not land but kingdom. All are to give of whatever they have, even as God gives. That means to love enemies, to turn the other cheek, to give not only your coat but the shirt off your back as well. The logic of the jubilee kingdom is a logic that goes beyond loving people who love us, or lending in hope of return with profit. To love enemies, to pray for those who curse us, to lend without hope of return, and to be merciful as God is merciful is what the jubilee kingdom means for the majority of the followers of Jesus, who do not possess debts, slaves, or land.

The jubilee kingdom proclamation of Jesus thus intends

to reverse the whole pattern of life that focuses on self. Such a task is enormously difficult, for it is human nature to observe the splinter in another's eye and never notice the plank in one's own. The revolutionary temptation is, of course, to keep the attention of the crowds focused solely on the people in power, on their sins, and on their oppression of the poor. Jesus does proclaim: Woe to you who are rich; you are having your consolation now! But he also examines the life of each disciple, rich or poor, with the images of the jubilee kingdom.

In this sermon, then, Jesus turns the proclamation of the jubilee kingdom toward himself and his movement. The proclaimers of the jubilee kingdom must live in jubilee. Like Jesus, they must be willing to pray for the coming kingdom, for daily bread, and for forgiveness. The revolutionary violence of the Maccabees and their followers, the Zealots, is clearly rejected. The jubilee kingdom may not be forced by holy war, for jubilee springs out of the love that is owed to brothers and sisters. That love is a merciful love, a love like God's love for us. The requirement of the covenant is clear: "You shall love your neighbor as yourself."

Jesus also demands that the religious leadership understand themselves in a new way. The religious authorities neglect the cause of the poor and accommodate themselves to the present regime. They reduce religion to ritual and forget justice. They observe the splinter in the other person's eye and never notice the plank in their own. Jesus and his movement are therefore greeted with hostility by the authorities, both religious and political, for he is proclaiming a radical revision of the economic, political, and religious communities in light of the ancient covenant.

Luke sketches the ministry in Galilee with stories of liberation from sickness, death, madness, hunger, and sin. These stories underline the reality that to be a proclaimer and bringer of a jubilee kingdom is to be given power and glory by the crowds. Jesus is tempted to exploit that power by using it to overthrow the present social order. But the jubilee kingdom is not only social justice, it is also the gift of forgiveness given in response to God's gift. Therefore it cannot be turned into a holy war, not even a war for a just cause. If violence is renounced, if the other cheek is turned, and the kingdom is nevertheless proclaimed, then the cross is indeed a certain end.

So Jesus begins to teach his disciples that he is to suffer, and that if anyone wants to follow him, that person must also renounce self and take up the cross every day. Eight days later, on the mount of transfiguration, this perspective is confirmed by the renewal of Jesus' commission. The voice from heaven speaks a second time: "This is my Son, the Chosen One. Listen to him" (Luke 9:35). Shortly after this, "when everyone was full of admiration for all he did," Jesus reminds his disciples again of the cross. Those who are the established powers will maintain themselves by exercising the established forms of violence.

The section of the Gospel from 9:51 to 19:44 is primarily a collection of Jesus' teachings, which Luke sets within a journey to Jerusalem. Here on the road the theme of jubilee kingdom repeatedly reverses the contemporary way of understanding the world. A lawyer enquires into the meaning of *neighbor* in the command "You shall love your neighbor as yourself." Jesus' answer, the parable of the Good Samaritan, is a polar reversal of the ordinary world. The hearer is present in the action, to personally see, feel, and know the goodness of the Samaritan. But for Jesus' hearers Samaritans were evil. Thus the hearers imagine the unimaginable: a good Samaritan. In the world of the parable, the good clerics are evil, the evil Samaritan is good. But the parable not only deconstructs the ordinary world, it also reconstructs the new world of discipleship by giving new meaning to the term *neighbor*. No longer does neighbor mean "one of our own people." Neighbor is man or woman, Samaritan or Israelite, friend or enemy who is in need. In the kingdom of God, neighbor, Israelite, Samaritan, and even jubilee are radically re-visioned. Those who truly listen, who have ears to hear what is going on, experience the inbreak of the jubilee kingdom as they experience the world of the parable.[9]

Throughout the journey, Jesus continues to stress the
reign of God as a reversal of the ordinary world. Many of
the reversals are favorite Lukan themes. In telling the story
of Jesus' visit to the home of Mary and Martha, Luke underlines his understanding that women, just as men, are to
sit at the feet of Jesus as disciples. This "better part" is not
to be denied to Mary because she is a woman.

Jesus also returns again and again to the theme of jubilee. The rich fool pulls down his barns and builds bigger
ones to hold his abundant crops. No thoughts of the poor
or covenants or jubilees cross his mind. But God says to
him, "Fool! This very night the demand will be made for
your soul" (12:20). That is why, Jesus says, he is teaching
his disciples not to worry about what they shall eat or
wear. God will care for them, even as he has promised to
care for them in jubilee years when the land is not to be
sown (Lev. 25:20–22).

Likewise, the rich young ruler does not understand the
meaning of the jubilee kingdom. Filled with sadness, he
fails to take up Jesus' word, "Sell all that you have and
distribute to the poor, . . . and come, follow me." Jesus
points out how hard it is for a rich man to enter the kingdom of God; indeed, it is easier for a camel to pass through
the eye of the needle than for a rich man to enter the kingdom of God. The common judgment that the rich are
blessed of God is radically reversed (Luke 18:18–27).

Zacchaeus, a tax collector and a wealthy man, is the only
rich man in Luke's story who takes up jubilee. When Jesus
calls him down from the tree, he pledges to give half his
property to the poor and reimburse fourfold anyone he has
cheated. That a tax collector, despised as much or more
than a Samaritan, should be the one practitioner of jubilee
is Luke's final story of reversal on the road to Jerusalem.

The practice of jubilee is, of course, not the whole of
Jesus' proclamation, but it is for Jesus one of the clues to
the way God reigns, one of the ways of understanding what
it means to live in the kingdom of God. The forgiveness of
debts is the way that God acts, and when we live under his
rule we are to forgive debts as well. Jesus again presses

beyond the covenant demand of jubilee when he tells the story of the prodigal son. When the prodigal returns, after wasting his father's resources, he imagines that the most he can ask of his father is a job. But the father's imagination is much richer. He sees, runs, hugs, kisses, and celebrates. He is not responsive to the son's request that he provide the least possible acceptance. The father's forgiveness is unconditional; it is a genuinely new beginning; it is indeed a jubilee and a celebration. The celebrative character of the forgiveness does raise, however, the question of the reward due to faithfulness. The elder son asks, Ought not the faithful be blessed? And even if the wicked are no longer to be cursed, is it fair to greet their return with a celebration that is greater than the gifts given to the faithful? The parable does indeed reverse all our previous understandings of what it means to live under the rule of God (15:11–32).

The closing section of Luke's Gospel opens with the entry into Jerusalem and the first explicitly messianic language in the Gospel. But the messiah envisioned is a messiah of peace:

> *Blessings on the King who comes,*
> *in the name of the Lord!*
> Peace in heaven
> and glory in the highest heavens!
> Luke 19:38

Jesus drives out those who sell in the temple and begins teaching there every day. His teachings oppose the way the religious authorities accommodate themselves to political and economic forces. The people as a whole hang on Jesus' words, but the religious authorities are angry. In his response to the question of whether it is permissible to pay taxes to Caesar, he tells the authorities to give to Caesar what belongs to Caesar and to God what belongs to God. Sovereignty belongs to God. God allows rulers to reign. Herod and Pilate are not free to act as they please. Rulers, like everyone else, are to conform their actions to the action of God, which is made plain in the proclamation of the jubilee kingdom.

Jesus warns the disciples that the church must not imitate the politics of the world. The one who leads in the church must be servant of all. Even though it may seem that the only effective politics are those of the authorities or the revolutionaries, Jesus reminds them again that the kingdom is on its way as surely as the seeds grow and the harvest comes, as surely as the trees bud and summer follows. In the midst of all these signs the disciples are to live in the vision of the jubilee kingdom, for the close of the age is at hand. The cycle of Jesus' teaching in Jerusalem is thus one of opposition to the Jerusalem authorities and a warning to the disciples to remain steadfast.

In response to the public teaching of Jesus, the authorities take up the politics of the world and conspire to put him to death. The accusations they bring against him in his trials are appropriate to each authority. The religious authorities try him on charges of heresy, and the political authorities try him on political charges. He is accused of inciting people to revolt, opposing payment of taxes to Caesar, and claiming to be king. Throughout the scenes of trial and crucifixion, Jesus loves his enemies, does good to those who hate him, blesses those who curse him, and prays for those who treat him badly. To the one who slaps him on one cheek he presents the other cheek; he gives up both cloak and tunic and forgives his enemies all their debts, even the debt of violence that takes his life. Luke does not suggest that Jesus' death makes forgiveness of sinners possible. No, Jesus forgives because God has commissioned him to proclaim and establish the jubilee kingdom as a son who already lives under that rule. Jesus forgives because he is who he is, the son of God—whose way of ruling is displayed in Jesus.

The resurrection stories close the Gospel. Again, as in the opening story of the Gospel, the women believe, and they share the good news of the resurrection with the apostles. But to the men "this story of theirs seemed pure nonsense, and they did not believe them" (Luke 24:11).

On the road to Emmaus, Jesus joins two disciples and they discuss the things that have happened. The disciples express their grief in political language. Although throughout the story Jesus has done much that a political revolutionary would not do—heal the sick, forgive sins, and be himself one who forgives his enemies—still the political aspects of the theme of jubilee give credence to the disciple's political summary of his mission. Beginning with an interpretation of Moses, Jesus then teaches the two disciples the full meaning of his life. Jesus has inaugurated a new way of living together in personal, social, and political relationships. The new way is the way of the kingdom of God. The gift of the Spirit is Jesus' commission to inaugurate this kingdom, and his crucifixion and resurrection mark the culmination of the new regime in which all are invited to live.

Pauline Language of the Cross

As the community of the church spread beyond Palestine, the language of the jubilee kingdom was not as widely used. Other images came into play to express the way God reverses all human standards. Paul uses the metaphor of the cross to speak about the whole action of God in the life, death, and resurrection of Jesus. The language of the cross is crucial to Paul:

> For Christ did not send me to baptize, but to preach the Good News, and not to preach that in the terms of philosophy in which the crucifixion of Christ cannot be expressed.
> 1 Corinthians 1:17

For Paul the cross is a reversal of all human wisdom and all human standards. The proclamation of the cross brought upon Paul the sufferings that the proclamation of the kingdom brought upon Jesus. Both the disciples and the world had as much difficulty understanding Paul as they did understanding Jesus. The church at Corinth believed that its leaders should be learned, influential, even celebrities. In other words, the church wished to be a hierarchical community whose politics were like the politics of the world. Paul argues that the language of superstars is a language in which the crucifixion of Christ cannot be expressed. To live as a community under the sign of the cross is to live differently:

> Here we are, fools for the sake of Christ, while you are the learned men in Christ; we have no power, but you are influential; you are celebrities, we are nobodies. To this day, we go without food and drink and clothes; we are beaten and have no homes; we work for our living with our own hands. When we are cursed, we answer with a blessing, when we are hounded, we put up with it; we are insulted and we answer politely.
>
> 1 Corinthians 4:10–13

Paul returns to this argument with great emphasis in his letters to the churches in Philippi and Galatia. He urges the Philippians to put aside competition and conceit and replace them with an attitude that always thinks of other people's interests first (Phil. 2:3–5). He teaches the Galatians that "there are no more distinctions between Jew and Greek, slave and free, male and female, but all of you are one in Christ Jesus" (Gal. 3:28).

The task of the church among the nations is to be the community of people who are enabled to speak the truth to their society and to one another because they live not under the standards of the culture of which they are a part but under the sign of the cross. The political temptations of the church seem to be polar opposites. On the one hand, there is the temptation to withdraw to quietism, to attend primarily to the ritualistic tithing of mint and rue and overlook justice and the love of God. On the other hand, there is the temptation to become a community whose politics are indistinguishable from the politics of the nation in which it lives, and thus to speak a language in which the cross of Christ cannot be expressed.

Self, World, and Self-deception in Biblical Story

This brief sketch of some prominent stories within the biblical narrative helps us see what kind of world is portrayed in the biblical story. In that world all action, both of God and of Israel, is to be understood in light of the promise "I shall be your God, you shall be my people." Through this interaction between God and God's people, we come to know both the character of God and the character of God's people.

First, the covenantal stories tell of God who acts in these ways: promises land, rescues from Egypt, sustains in wilderness, and gives the gift of land. All these stories about God's activity are specifications of the promise "I will be your God." We come to know who God is: namely, the God who is always willing to begin anew. God begins anew with Adam and Eve, Abraham, Isaac, Jacob, Joseph, Moses, the prophets, and Jesus. The forgiveness that Jesus proclaims and lives is paradigmatic of God's initiatives. That initiative for renewal consequently gives us hope, for it tells us that our endings are not fixed by fate. We do not struggle through life facing impersonal powers unable to respond to the human condition. On the contrary, we are people who live before the face of the God who continually begins anew with us.

Second, the covenant is a promise that God will stay in character and continue to be this kind of person. Since that is who God is, then the people of the covenant community increasingly sense that their lives are influenced by God's providence. Even though Joseph is sold into slavery, thrown into prison, and exiled from his family, he can proclaim it is all done under the watchful, caring eye of God. Jesus, as he faces the cross, declares that he is going in the way that was determined, and that he is willing to drink the cup that the Father has set before him.

Third, when Jesus inaugurates the new order of jubilee, it is especially God's forgiveness that constitutes the people of God. Forgiveness is required of the one who receives Yahweh's forgiveness. Jesus puts it simply: "Be perfect, even as your heavenly Father is perfect." On one hand, forgiveness is strongly connected to earlier themes about forgiving debtors and liberating the enslaved. On the other hand, being forgiven is prerequisite to being free to respond anew to the covenant summons. Forgiveness creates a genuinely new beginning, for it opens the possibility that we can become other than we are, that we can be persons who develop and grow.

Forgiveness, then, has the character of a gift that reverses earlier gifts in the biblical story. Reversal itself is not a new theme with Jesus. It was present in all the ways God began again across the whole story. However, in Jesus' ministry, the theme of reversal takes center stage. His teachings, parables, actions, and finally the cross and the resurrection are witnesses to the way God's action reverses both the world of the culture and the disciples' complacent confidence that they fully understand the ways of God.[10]

In summary, the dominant image of self and world that emerges from biblical story is one of gift and response. Life, in all its varied expressions, its blessings and sufferings, is given to us by God. Since we have received both self and world as gifts from God, we ourselves are to be gift-givers. We are to care even as we have been cared for, remembering the weak, the poor, and the oppressed even as we have been remembered. When we do not respond faithfully, we are offered yet another gift, forgiveness, which opens the door to a new beginning, with self, with others, and with God.

The tragedy is that the self that appropriates gifts from God, responds faithfully, and makes new beginnings is also the self that tends inveterately toward self-deception. Self-deception occurs when we persistently use a cover story to avoid telling the truth about some aspect of how we relate to our world. It is not just the inspired invention of a cover story or a single rehearsal of it. Self-deception is a *policy* of avoiding the real story. Self-deception appears in biblical story when the characters persistently avoid accounting for actions that do not conform to the covenant.

Paul's letters to the church at Corinth serve as an excellent example of how Christians struggle with self-deception. In face of the plain teaching and clear example of Jesus, the Corinthians fuss, feud, and boast about who is number one in the church, who is most spiritual, and who has the right to to exercise dominance over the others. Paul continually reminds them of the cross. But the only language of leadership that the Corinthians use is the language of the nations, which embodies a philosophy of politics in which the crucifixion of Christ cannot be expressed. In the case of the Corinthian Christians, self-deception is a policy of not making explicit to themselves and others those images through which they know themselves and that guide their action and then comparing those images to the story of the cross.

Paul's letters to the Corinthians attempt to teach them the skill necessary to overcome self-deception. This skill is dependent upon the world-shaping story used. First, the story must have power to convince hearers that it is true. For a story to have such power it must enable us to think in a fresh way, to continually hope that we are about to break out of our old inadequate way of interpreting life into a new vision of reality. Second, the story must have the resources within itself to move against the endemic tendency toward self-deception. The biblical story does both. It presents a vision of reality opposed to self-centered perspectives. The biblical story continually calls us beyond self-serving exploitation of the land or of other people and into covenantal existence. This story of the denial of self for the sake of both God and the people of God rings true. Those stories that give rein to endless self-aggrandizement, that end in the holocausts of history, ring false.

But as the Corinthians, the rich young man, King David, and the rich fool all make so clear, we can readily become involved in self-deception even when we claim to live in the biblical story. We can avoid spelling out what we are doing. We can hide under a cover story and not be able to see how it obscures or even betrays the original story. The stories of self-deception in the biblical story, however, are resources for the skill of spelling out what we are really doing. Stories such as the parable of the prodigal son, with its deft characterization of younger son, father, and older son, call our attention to the way actions shape character. The story asks each one of us, Who am I becoming? In his

letters to the Corinthian Christians Paul uses the story of
the cross to teach them how to inquire into the character of
their own actions. Since the story of Jesus, the cross, and
the equality of all in Christ is such a radical reversal of the
story of the leaders of the Corinthian church, Paul's use of
the cross story enables the Corinthians to re-examine
themselves, to spell out what they are doing, and to acknowledge their self-deception.

Conclusion

As we noted at the outset of this chapter, the biblical
story was a principal force in the creation of the American
culture. The biblical understanding of covenant gave Winthrop and many of those who followed him an interpretative framework for their actions and their sufferings. It
was, of course, not the only story that was shaping American experience. The Enlightenment story of progress and
the mission-of-America story were at hand. These stories
and the biblical story combine and compete in many ways
in the American experience. But such a fusion, and confusion, of stories is commonplace in the biblical story itself.
The story of the people of God is always a story told in the
midst of other stories: the story of Pharaoh, the story of
Baal, the stories of the nations, the stories told in the languages of Corinth and Rome. To live in the biblical story is
to live in conflicting stories. But, more than that, it is to
live with the resources that are required to deal with self-
deception. Therefore, we can live in a world where truth is
possible. One of the skills the biblical story teaches is the
skill of seeing the differences among stories and to understand what is at stake in those differences. To this task we
now turn.

3

The Gospel of Success in America

During the eighteenth century, the Enlightenment story of progress slowly gained power as a cultural narrative in America. By the nineteenth century it was challenging biblical story as the primary vision of self and world. As the eighteenth century opened, American intellectuals began to participate in the European Enlightenment. In the second half of the century, the Americans turned from their interest in the English Enlightenment to the more skeptical French Enlightenment, whose thought supported the American interest in deism and revolutionary politics. Once the revolutionary period was past, the pragmatic themes of the Scottish Enlightenment became important to Americans. The Scots trusted in a rational universe, in clear and certain moral judgments, and in progress. In this period, the most important ideas of the American Enlightenment were assimilated into the wider American culture. Moralism—the belief that accepted moral dogmas were part of the framework of the universe—became an important part of the American worldview.[1]

The Public Religion

Benjamin Franklin and Thomas Jefferson were the best known of the American intellectuals who embraced the Enlightenment view of the world. They accepted the Newtonian presupposition that the universe is orderly and law-governed. They also placed great trust in reason. Henry

Steele Commager has pointed out that for Franklin and Jefferson,

> Reason could penetrate to and master the laws of Nature and of God, and . . . it could persuade men to conform to them, not only in philosophy and ethics, but in politics, economy, law, education, even in art and literature.[2]

Because of their dependence on reason, Franklin and Jefferson understood religion in a new way. To them, the mind was more important than the heart; reason carried greater weight than faith. Public virtue mattered more than private salvation; morals meant more than grace. They considered that Jesus had produced the best system of morals and religion the world had ever seen, but they thought the church had obscured the simple message of Jesus with complex doctrines. The interest of Franklin and Jefferson in morals and public virtue led them to argue that the primary duty of churches was to produce a common morality based on reason. Therefore, they sought to develop a universal creed or public religion.[3]

Franklin and Jefferson were joined by Washington and Madison and other politically active Americans in encouraging the development of a public religion. This public religion—sometimes called "the democratic faith" or "civil religion"—was first advocated by Franklin in 1749. Franklin proposed that the youth in Philadelphia be educated in the public religion. The creed of such a religion, Franklin thought, ought to contain the "essentials of every known religion":

> That there is one God, who made all things.
> That he governs the world by his providence.
> That he ought to be worshiped by adoration, prayer, and thanksgiving.
> But that the most acceptable service to God is doing good to man.
> That the soul is immortal.
> And that God will certainly reward virtue and punish vice, either here or hereafter.[4]

The way Jefferson speaks of God in the Declaration of Independence is in basic agreement with Franklin but greatly enriches the meaning of public religion. In its opening section, the Declaration affirms that a people is entitled to a "separate and equal station" by "the Laws of Nature and of Nature's God." The heart of the Enlightenment faith is then stated in the creed: "We hold these truths to be self-evident, that all men are created equal, that they are endowed by their Creator with certain unalienable Rights; that among these are Life, Liberty and the pursuit of Happiness." Jefferson was not the inventor of these principles. With other Enlightenment thinkers, he assumed that universal equality and inalienable rights are an integral part of the fundamental law of the universe. From the perspective of such a faith, the American Revolution is nothing less than a reasonable response to the "Laws of Nature and of Nature's God."

The Declaration's last two references to God, an appeal to the "Supreme Judge of the world" and to the "protection of Divine Providence," have more in common with the biblical than the Enlightenment heritage. Nevertheless, such language makes it clear that the God of the civil religion is much more related to reason, order, law, equality, and rights than to forgiveness, faith, or love.

During his presidential term, Jefferson continued to display his interest in public religion by writing a universal gospel, *The Life and Morals of Jesus of Nazareth.* Jefferson's gospel was a patchwork of stories and teachings from the four Gospels. Jefferson selected passages that were simple, moral, and nonmiraculous, for he wanted his gospel to appeal to reason.

Jefferson also translated the words of the Puritans about a sense of mission and covenant into images congenial to public religion. Martin Marty has pointed out that, as Winthrop had once imagined the eyes of the world were on New England, Jefferson was certain all the world would look to America for light. He declared that the Republic was "the only monument of human rights, and the sole depository of

the sacred fire of freedom and self-government." America
was a "chosen country," and her people were "enlightened
by a benign religion."[5]

The organized advocacy of this early phase of public
religion was sustained by Enlightenment intellectuals
throughout the forty years of the revolutionary generation.
At first public religion did not often speak to the needs of
the common people of America. Nevertheless, its institutional forms were an important factor in the shaping of
American culture. The Declaration was the creed of the
public religion. The public school, with its celebration of
America as God's new nation, became the parochial school
of the public religion. The presidential addresses con-
tained formal references to public religion. Washington's
first inaugural address served as an example for the presidents who followed. Washington declared:

> No people can be bound to acknowledge and adore the Invis-
> ible Hand which conducts the affairs of man more than those
> of the United States.
>   . . . The preservation of the sacred fire of liberty and the
> destiny of the republican model of government are justly
> considered, perhaps, as *deeply,* as *finally* staked on the exper-
> iment intrusted to the hands of the American people.[6]

Some popular American poetry and hymns became the
psalms of the public religion, and aspects of the legal tradition continued to celebrate it. Through its institutional
forms, then, the public religion carried the themes of the
Enlightenment into the nineteenth century and wove them
into the story of America.

The Assimilation of the Enlightenment

The Enlightenment story of progress also had a deep impact on the American vision of self and world because it
was assimilated to the biblical story in the early nineteenth
century. As a result of the Second Great Awakening,
Americans had come to believe that morality rests on
faith, not reason. This widespread turn to faith as the basis

of morality was interpreted by many as a cultural rejection of the Enlightenment's confidence in reason. However, the more crucial issue was the content of the faith. What was accepted by faith was very similar to what had been affirmed by reason. Americans, reflecting upon their experience with the earlier images of the public religion, created a full-bodied democratic faith.[7]

According to Ralph Henry Gabriel, the democratic faith consisted of three doctrines. First, nineteenth-century Americans believed in the moral law. They were convinced that society, its customs and its institutions, were founded on a fundamental law that governed both nature and society. Evangelical Christians spoke of the fundamental law in biblical language. Those whose understanding of self and world was shaped by the Enlightenment tradition spoke of the natural law. Most people blended two familiar ideas—the will of God from the biblical tradition and the doctrine of natural rights from the Declaration of Independence. This moral law was the foundation upon which the Constitution itself rested. That the American government rested on constitutionalism was, for the majority of citizens, evidence that America was faithful to the moral law, which was given by God, and as Ralph Waldo Emerson said in 1836, "lies at the center of nature and radiates to the circumference."[8]

Second, Americans believed in the doctrine of the free and responsible individual. Free individuals were those who had the power to shape their own lives. In political life, the ballot was imagined as the instrument of power through which individuals were the ultimate governors of the nation. In personal life, a person could succeed in America by industriousness. But the individual was called to exercise power responsibly: that is, in accordance with the moral law. If the free individual exercised power according to the moral law, then both the individual and the community would progress. The doctrine of the calling— the conviction that each person was called to a life work that served both self and community—was considered part of the moral law and tempered individualism with a concern for community. Thus progress was considered to be a virtue because it emerged from the discovery of and faithful adherence to the laws that govern the universe. The doctrine of the free individual was connected to the doctrine of the fundamental law by the idea of progress. To Americans who held such a faith, the advance of both civilization and the individual was also the advance of virtue.[9]

Third, Americans believed in the mission of America. The mission of America was the conviction that the United States was to serve as an example of God's plan for the world, as proof that a people can govern themselves in peace and justice. The idea of mission gave a sense of meaning to Americans, for it invested the performance of ordinary civic duties with world significance and bound the diverse peoples called American into one people with a common cause.

Out of the impact of the Enlightenment upon American culture two different cultural stories emerged in the nineteenth century. The story of the mission of America emphasized a communal rather than an individual reality, for it spoke not of the task of the individual but of the task of America among the nations. In the fifth chapter we will trace the meaning of the mission of America through an examination of America's wars.

But the story that resounded most loudly in the daily life of individuals was the story of success, a story that emphasized the ability of each individual to make personal progress. This story took up the themes of the fundamental law and the free individual. The wise and good individual lived in faithful adherence to the laws that governed the world, whether those laws were of nature or of God. The utilitarian nature of such virtue was emphasized by the direct connection that was made between economic success and the moral life. In the "gospel of success," the moral man became an economic success.

The gospel of success was the personal side of the Enlightenment story of progress. The exemplars of this story were Benjamin Franklin and Andrew Carnegie. Nineteenth-century America applauded the success of these two men and published and republished their books, essays, and autobiographies. Benjamin Franklin taught the "way to wealth" as if it were the way to the kingdom of God. Andrew Carnegie believed his success was one more demonstration of the truth of nature's law. In order to understand this gospel of success, we shall first turn to Franklin and those who understood him to be a representative type of the American people. We shall then take up Carnegie and his view of self and world.

Benjamin Franklin and the Self-made Man

In 1904 Max Weber wrote his classic essay *The Protestant Ethic and the Spirit of Capitalism*. He quoted at length from "Advice to a Young Tradesman" and "Hints to Those That Would Be Rich," by Benjamin Franklin. Franklin advised young men to

> Remember, that *time* is money. He that can earn ten shillings a day by his labour, and goes abroad, or sits idle, one half of that day, though he spends but sixpence during his diversion or idleness, ought not to reckon *that* the only expense; he has really spent, or rather thrown away, five shillings besides.
>
> Remember that *credit* is money. . . . The most trifling actions that affect a man's credit are to be regarded. The sound of your hammer at five in the morning, or eight at night, heard by a creditor, makes him easy six months longer; but if he sees you at a billiard table, or hears your voice at a tavern, when you should be at work, he sends for his money the next day; demands it, before he can receive it, in a lump.[10]

The quality that interests—even amazes—Weber in Franklin is not that he teaches young men how to make money but that he preaches an ethic, an ethos, a *summum bonum*. This highest good is to succeed in one's "calling," whatever that vocation might be. In a capitalist society, Weber notes, success is measured primarily by money. Money-making is no longer simply a necessity in American society, something that everyone must do in order to keep body and soul together and to be able to enjoy a bit of life free from the privations of want. No, to make money is to succeed, to be worthwhile, and to give evidence that one's character is well formed and rightfully exercised. Franklin, therefore, serves as an exemplar of American society.

Weber was right to select Benjamin Franklin as an exemplar of the success orientation, for Franklin's writings on success and his *Autobiography* had been widely read in America for well over a century. Franklin was seen as both an example to be followed in order to gain personal success and as a representative type of the American people, who were rising even as Franklin did. Young men who aspired to wealth or position were admonished to read Franklin's writings. Millionaires such as Thomas Mellon testified to the influence of Franklin on their lives. Mellon read Franklin's *Autobiography* on the farm in 1928. Mellon was only fourteen, but Franklin fired him with ambition:

> I had not before imagined any other course of life superior to farming, but the reading of Franklin's life led me to question this view. For so poor and friendless a boy to be able to become a merchant or a professional man had before seemed an impossibility; but here was Franklin, poorer than myself, who by industry, thrift and frugality had become learned and wise, and elevated to wealth and fame. The maxims of "Poor Richard" exactly suited my sentiments . . . I regard the reading of Franklin's *Autobiography* as the turning point of my life.[11]

In his later life, having amassed a fortune, Mellon purchased a thousand copies of Franklin's *Autobiography,* which he gave to young men as an encouragement to follow both Franklin and himself. Franklin's life had become a master image for the cultural narrative of progress.

Franklin's *Autobiography* is a somewhat rambling, sometimes witty, often ironic presentation by Franklin of himself as a character. Franklin's use of irony both charms and cautions the reader. The charm is needed. Franklin's style tends toward self-righteousness, for he is encouraging us to imitate him. The caution urges us to think again about who Franklin is, for it reminds us that Franklin is committed to live a reasonable life, but he has some skepticism about the power of reason; that he urges industry and frugality in work, but he retires at age forty-two and lives the anything-but-frugal life in Paris; that he gives advice that seems to envision an orderly and stable world, but he lives in the bustling, energetic disorder of eighteenth-century America; that he preaches prudence and carefulness, and he makes revolution; finally, that he speaks endlessly about how to grow rich, but he leaves his business and spends most of his adult life in public service.

Franklin is as many-faceted as the American character itself, and it is therefore difficult to attempt to capture him from a single perspective. Even though his own life reflects such ironies, Franklin writes so as to persuade his reader that character and success are related as cause and effect. Franklin argues that our destiny is in our own hands, for each one of us is able to develop her or his own character, and a good character brings a good reward.[12]

In the *Autobiography,* Franklin presents himself as a simple country boy, who with much hard work and plain virtue has made good in Philadelphia. Franklin carefully constructs the scene of his entry into the city. He arrives dirty, fatigued, and hungry from the long journey from his native Boston. Munching on a roll, he walks up Market Street, passing by the Read home, where his future wife sees him. She thinks he makes "a most awkward, ridiculous appearance." Franklin takes us back to this scene a number of times in order to contrast his low beginnings with the heights he has reached.[13]

The low beginnings were the result of the lack of design that characterized his life before 1726. He did not discipline himself. Instead, he quarreled with his brother and father, left Boston secretly and against the wishes of his family, borrowed money, and spent it with his employer Keimer and his friend Ralph on drink and "low women." Encouraged by the governor to open his own printing shop in Philadelphia, Franklin went to London with Ralph to purchase printing equipment. When the letters of credit

promised by the governor failed to arrive, Franklin was
without funds and was forced to find work as a printer.
Instead of saving money for his equipment, however, he
regularly exhausted his funds and himself in going to
"places of amusement" with Ralph, and they just "rubbed
on from hand to mouth." Franklin disregarded his engage-
ment to Miss Read and angered Ralph by attempting to
seduce "Mrs. T," who had been living with Ralph. With
the loss of the friendship, Franklin changed to a job at a
larger printing house and tried unsuccessfully to raise
funds for the return voyage. At last, a merchant offered to
lend him money for the journey home.

On board ship Franklin reconsidered his freethinker
conviction that vice and virtue were empty distinctions.
Because freethinkers wronged others without the least
compunction, Franklin concluded that even though his
freethinker doctrine might be true, it was not useful, and
what was not useful was not reasonable. Practical reason,
based on experience, was what enabled one to live a useful
life. Philosophical precepts or religious commandments
made sense only if they encouraged persons to do what was
good for them or to refrain from doing what was bad for
them. This persuasion allowed Franklin to rationally use
the advice of scripture to help him live a more useful life.

As he reflected on his life, it was plain to him that truth,
sincerity, and integrity in his relationships with other persons were of the utmost usefulness. He therefore formed
four resolutions so he might "live in all respects like a
rational creature": (1) to be extremely frugal, (2) to en-
deavor to speak the truth and to aim at sincerity, "the
most amiable excellence in a rational being," (3) to apply
himself industriously and patiently to his business as the
surest means of plenty, and (4) to speak no ill but to speak
all the good known of everybody.[14]

The resolutions were the mark of Franklin's conversion
to the moral life. Like others before him who intended to
lead a new life, however, he soon desired to do more and
entered upon the project of arriving at moral perfection. It
was more difficult than he imagined, so he contrived an

experimental method to habituate himself to a list of thirteen virtues. Although he never attained the perfection he had wanted, he concluded that because of the effort he was a better and happier man.

In the first section of *Autobiography*, Franklin, like Augustine, reflected on the depths to which he had fallen and confessed his sins (which Franklin calls "errata," the printer's term for mistakes). But that was now behind him. Franklin forsook his former ways, his former companions, and his former doctrines. He took up only useful doctrines, useful companions, and useful ways. The perils he met were no longer the perils of his own inner confusion and waywardness, but the perils of the outside world.

Returning to Keimer's print shop in Philadelphia, Franklin acted on his resolutions. A new fellow worker, Meredith, had a father who advanced the capital that enabled Franklin and Meredith to open their own print shop. When Meredith turned out to be like Ralph, spending his substance on drink and in places of amusement, two other friends offered to lend Franklin money. He accepted the offer, bought Meredith out, and became the sole proprietor.

Although he formed his "ingenious acquaintances into a club of mutual improvement," Franklin allowed nothing to interfere with work. He worked late, even until eleven at night, to finish printing work he had promised. His neighbors noticed, and at the merchants' "Every Night Club" Franklin's long hours and hard work were commented upon. In order to secure his credit and character as a tradesman he took care to be industrious in both reality and appearance. He carried his own supplies through the streets of Philadelphia in a wheelbarrow to show that he was a sober, industrious worker. He avoided the tavern lest his reputation be compromised. He was exact in his accounts, so that other merchants would trust him. He established a newspaper, became postmaster, sent his newspaper through the mail, and at last began to prosper. He paid back his debts and married Miss Read, who worked alongside him in the shop. Thus he atoned for some of his "errata."

About this time Franklin began to publish his almanac

under the name of Richard Saunders. He filled all the open spaces with Poor Richard sayings. The sayings were proverbs that connected industry and frugality to wealth and virtue. With the publication of *Poor Richard*, Franklin completed his transformation into Max Weber's exemplar of the capitalist ethic.

In his *Autobiography*, Franklin, like the Puritan preachers of his time, commonly appended a moral to the story of a peril. Franklin was certain the dangers of hunger or debtor's prison were real for the person who transgressed the fundamental economic laws. So when Keimer lost his postmastership because of negligence in his accounts and thus lost his paper and finally his printing business, Franklin wrote the moral:

> Thus he suffered greatly from his neglect in due accounting; and I mention it as a lesson to those young men who may be employed in managing affairs for others, that they should always render accounts, and make remittances, with great clearness and punctuality.[15]

He wrote of his own thrift, industry, and honesty in order to remind his readers that those who exercised the virtue of industry were amply rewarded according to the fundamental economic laws. The reminders serve their purpose, for even before the reader has finished the *Autobiography*, he or she has realized that Franklin has been telling the story of his life, his age, and his country as the story of the self-made man.

To Franklin, the self-made man was the man of virtue. He was a man of reason who understood the wider vision of a rationally ordered universe in which a reasonable people could steadily progress. The economic laws by which a person or society could advance were part of that rational world. Franklin was convinced that disciplined adherence to the laws of economic progress led to financial success. But financial success was more than just a reward in itself. It was also evidence that a person was living a virtuous life: that is, a life lived in harmony with the fundamental law of the universe.

Robert Bellah notes that though the model of Benjamin Franklin, the self-made man, loomed large in the consciousness of nineteenth-century Americans, two aspects of reality mitigated the radical individualism of the era. First, although the major emphasis was placed on male roles, the achievement of farmers and artisans depended on women, who played a vital economic role. So Franklin argued that a good wife was necessary if a man was to succeed. Second, the world in which the self-made man lived was the face-to-face community of the town. The communal ethos of the town kept alive the vision of work as calling that served the common good. As the Second Great Awakening reinforced the biblical image of the calling, Franklin's method of gathering a group of citizens together to found a library, sweep and light the streets, create a volunteer fire department, establish a school, or reform the morals of the town became part of the texture of the American community. As noted above, the idea that each citizen was called to serve the community became part of the democratic faith and tempered the radical individualism of the self-made man.[16]

However, the biblical image of the calling is radically reoriented by Franklin. It is reason, not God, that calls persons to labor for the common good. Just as individuals ought to do what is useful to secure their credit and character as tradesmen, so together the people of the town ought to do what is useful to enhance the life of the town. As Weber points out, Franklin translates the Puritan notion of the calling from the language of biblical story into the language of the Enlightenment.[17]

The contrast between Franklin and the Puritans who are still rooted in the biblical understanding of calling can be seen in *Essays to Do Good,* by Cotton Mather, a Puritan contemporary of Franklin. For Mather, the calling is a person's profession, trade, or task within the community. As such, it is part of God's organization of the social life of Christians. Since all Christian activity is to be activity for the greater glory of God, so then must the daily work be done as unto God. The calling in which a Christian works must therefore serve to support or enhance the life of the community. In this sense, all callings are holy callings. The Christian rejoices in work that serves the community and shuns work that does not. Faithful performance of work that serves is faithful praise to God.[18]

Franklin approves of Mather's *Essays to Do Good*, for to Franklin they contain much good advice on how each person can be "useful" in his or her calling. But when the world is no longer the world of providence but has become the world of the Enlightenment, the character of the calling undergoes a radical change. For Mather, one's actions are useful to God and neighbor within the context of the covenant. For Franklin, one's actions are useful in enabling one to rise from poverty to affluence in a world that encourages progress.[19]

It is the intense emphasis on usefulness that separates Franklin from the Puritans of his time. The outer covenant of works, in which we are useful to one another in the community, makes sense to the Puritans only if there is an inner covenant of faith. From Winthrop to Mather, life is always seen through the twofold vision of the covenant—an inner and an outer covenant, life as God sees it and life as we see it. Life is always more than it appears to be. To say that it is the providence of God that has placed a person in a calling or a people in a land is to speak of God's action, and the intentions of God are not fully known. The Puritans believe, however, that the depths of God's covenant purposes are displayed in the logic of the biblical narrative. But the logic of narrative can never be reduced to the language of usefulness.

Although Franklin's character is, as we have noted, multifaceted, he is at last a man of "single vision," to use William Blake's term. Like other Enlightenment thinkers, Franklin is a rationalist. The universe is intelligible, harmonious, and rational—in short, a vast mechanism. Franklin does not suppose that we have yet understood all the universe is, and his irony, even about the power of reason itself, is a caution. But he does believe that we can reduce the biblical stories, which display the character of

God, God's people, and the world, to useful laws that encourage progress in all of life. Faithful adherence to such laws will enable the individual and the community to become a moral and financial success.[20]

Franklin's pragmatic rationalism was widely adopted in America in the nineteenth century. The image of usefulness that was so important to Franklin met the needs of the expanding commercial and industrial economy. Both technical advances and willing useful workers were needed to exploit the wealth of an undeveloped continent. The American penchant for practical achievement diminished appreciation for other dimensions of human experience. The person of good character was the one, according to the stories of the McGuffey *Eclectic Readers,* who knew that the individual was the architect of his or her own fortune. Hard work and frugality were required of the individual who wished to climb the heights of achievement. Success in life was not a matter of being given the gifts of talent or opportunity, but success attended the common virtue of hard work:

> You will see issuing from the walls of the same college, nay, sometimes from the bosom of the same family, two young men, of whom one will be admitted to be a genius of high order, the other scarcely above the point of mediocrity; yet you will see the genius sinking and perishing in poverty, obscurity, and wretchedness; while, on the other hand, you will observe the mediocre plodding his slow but sure way up the hill of life, gaining steadfast footing at every step, and mounting, at length, to eminence and distinction, an ornament to his family, a blessing to his country.
>
> Now, whose work is this? Manifestly their own. They are the architects of their respective fortunes.[21]

Generations of children, nurtured on the McGuffey *Readers,* were schooled in its virtuous single vision of life. The recurring theme of the biblical story that we have been bound by the gift of God into community with God and one another was radically transformed. But as Bellah has noted, although the constraints of community were weakened, they did not disappear. The moral life of the towns and small cities of America still called individuals to a concern for the common good.

Andrew Carnegie and the "Gospel of Wealth"

In the last quarter of the nineteenth century, however, American society passed through a profound transformation. The industrial revolution produced a new, economically integrated society by the turn of the century. A new institution, the corporation, extended the control of a small group of investors over large numbers of employees, many of whom lived and worked at a great distance from corporate headquarters. Robert Bellah points out that by means of the corporation, the new self-made man, the captain of industry, could ignore the constraints of community and gain power and prestige by economic means alone. The age produced an untrammeled pursuit of wealth without regard to earlier concerns for justice or the common welfare. Success in America came to be equated with success in making money. The new captains of industry justified their actions in terms of what was later called the "gospel of wealth."[22]

The gospel of wealth was given its most famous articulation by Andrew Carnegie in 1889 in an article in the *North American Review* entitled "Wealth." Carnegie, of course, did not invent the gospel of wealth, but he gave expression to a widely held point of view. For Franklin, and the majority who embraced the American democratic faith, the free and responsible individual lived in harmony with the fundamental law. By the time of Carnegie's article, many persons made the connection between character and success in terms of the expanding middle class and its free enterprise system. It seemed to the middle class (who now considered themselves the quintessential Americans) that the American way of free enterprise and democracy was providing a steady increase in the economic, material, and even spiritual well-being of the people. The literature of the time abounded in stories of how persons of good character, exercising industry and frugality, always overcame great odds and succeeded. Likewise, the people as a whole—the nation itself—had overcome great odds, even the Civil War, and was growing richer day by day. It seemed self-evident that America was leading the advance of civilization.

To be sure, upheavals were challenging the complacent outlook of the period. There was discontent smoldering in agriculture and labor. The railroad strikes, beginning in 1877, led to pitched battles between workers and militia; the Haymarket Square bombing in 1886 killed eight policemen and injured a score of persons; in the 1892 strike at the Carnegie Steel Plant in Homestead, Pennsylvania, ten were killed and sixty wounded in a pitched battle. Eighteen ninety-three was a year of bitter depression, and 1894 saw the Pullman Palace Car strike. Still, most of the middle class remained optimistic about the prospects of success in America. It was in the context of such an understanding of success that Carnegie wrote "Wealth."[23]

Carnegie begins the article by welcoming the changes wrought by the industrial revolution. Even though there is a great difference between the situations of the rich and the poor, still it is better than the old days when everyone lived in squalor. The working class is today better off than the peasants of old. The fundamental laws of modern society do not provide equal wealth for everyone; they are, nevertheless, the best and most valuable that humanity has devised. The laws are four: (1) individualism, (2) private property, (3) accumulation of wealth, and (4) competition.[24]

Carnegie points out that the price society pays for the law of competition is great, but its advantages are greater still. It is hard for the individual, but it is best for the race, because it ensures the survival of the fittest. The people who have a special talent for organization and management create capital. Capital fuels the great industrial machine of the new order, which lifts laborer and capitalist alike. Unfortunately, the employer of thousands is bound by the law of competition to the lowest labor wages possible. Nevertheless, the capitalist, because of his peculiar talent, is promoting the best interest of the whole race, for competition ensures that the fittest survive. Again, of necessity, the fittest benefit from the law of accumulation of wealth.

According to Carnegie, the objections of anarchists and socialists to these four laws are out of order. Anyone who studies history will be forced to accept the truth that civilization itself is constructed on faith in the sacredness of private property. The laborer must have a right to his few dollars in a savings bank and the capitalist to his millions if the race is to go forward. To demand that individuals labor for the brotherhood of all rather than for themselves would necessitate changing human nature itself. To attempt to cast aside the law of individualism is to attempt revolution, and thus fly in the face of all that science teaches about the way nature perfects each species through evolution.

> We might as well urge the destruction of the highest existing type of man because he failed to reach our ideal as to favor the destruction of Individualism, Private Property, the Law of Accumulation of Wealth, and the Law of Competition; for these are the highest results of human experience, the soil in which society so far has produced the best fruit. . . . They are . . . like the highest type of man, the best and most valuable of all that humanity has yet accomplished.[25]

The man of wealth, however, has a duty to the rest of society. He is to administer his surplus wealth as a trust for his poorer brethren. In bestowing charity, the main consideration must be to help those who will help themselves. Neither the individual nor the race is improved by almsgiving, for it rewards vice rather than relieves virtue. Thus the rich should establish parks, means of recreation, art museums, public libraries. This does the poor the most lasting good. Carnegie concludes that this "is the true Gospel concerning Wealth, obedience to which is destined to solve the problem of the Rich and the Poor, and to bring 'Peace on Earth, among men Good Will.' "[26]

Social Darwinism

In his *Autobiography* Carnegie restated the vision of the gospel of wealth. He affirmed that he was a disciple of

Herbert Spencer, an English sociologist who argued for Social Darwinism. In *On the Origin of Species,* Darwin had argued that species were strengthened through the process of the survival of the fittest. In *The Descent of Man* he applied the argument to human society. But Spencer pressed Darwin's logic to its extreme position. He argued that the survival of the fittest improved mankind in the long run, because in the natural order of things society regularly excreted its unhealthy, slow, and faithless members to leave more room for the deserving. Therefore, the "poverty of the incapable, the distresses that come upon the imprudent, the starvation of the idle, and those shoulderings aside of the weak by the strong, which leave so many in shallows and miseries are the decrees of a large farseeing benevolence," which was steadily improving society.[27]

Social Darwinism was accepted by much of the middle class because it reinforced the teachings of the Protestant ethic that had prevailed since Franklin. The Protestant ethic taught persons to be diligent in their callings. Self-discipline was a sign of good character. The person of good character inevitably succeeded. Social Darwinism encouraged persons to work wholeheartedly to ensure that they would be counted among the fittest who would survive and thus improve the race. Both the Protestant ethic and Social Darwinism thereby turned self-interest into a social good, and even the leaders of the church blurred the distinction between them.

Henry Ward Beecher, pastor of the Plymouth Congregational Church in Brooklyn from 1847 to 1887 and easily the most prominent preacher of his time, declared that "evolution is God's way of doing things." Bishop Lawrence of the Episcopal Church wrote an essay, "The Relation of Wealth to Morals," arguing that wealth comes only to moral persons, because persons could work with efficiency only when they worked in harmony with God's natural and spiritual laws. The secrets and wealth of nature were revealed only to those who disciplined themselves in right living and right thinking. Because of this harmony in

God's universe, godliness was in league with riches, and material prosperity was helping to make the national character sweeter, more joyous, more unselfish, and more Christlike.[28]

This point of view was taken up by those who were most successful, such as Carnegie. Yet the gospel of success that had been preached since Franklin had great attraction for those not yet successful. Against much experience, many were still convinced that if only they were a bit more self-disciplined and worked yet a little harder, they too could reach the pinnacle of success.

Carnegie's espousal of such a doctrine is understandable once he stood at the summit as the richest man in America. Like Franklin, he had arrived in a great city as a poverty-stricken boy. In a few years he had become rich beyond comprehension. Since he had rejected the Calvinist understanding of God's decrees and covenants taught by Scottish Presbyterianism, he was searching for some sense of order in the universe. He remembered in his *Autobiography* that, while he was reading the works of Darwin and Spencer,

> light came as in a flood and all was clear. Not only had I got rid of theology and the supernatural, but I had found the truth of evolution. "All is well since all grows better" became my motto, my true source of comfort.[29]

Carnegie was convinced that there is no conceivable end to man's march to perfection. "His face is turned to the light, he stands in the sun and looks upward."[30]

Note that Carnegie takes up the themes of the survival of the fittest in a positive sense. He does not agree with Spencer that society ought to prune its weaker members. He believes that those who are successful are simply those who have developed the rare ability to organize and manage effectively. Carnegie interprets his own success with the story of the survival of the fittest, but he still believes that he owes a debt to society. The wealthy man ought to return his wealth to society in a way that does the greatest service to all.

Self-deception and the Gospel of Success

The writings of Franklin and Carnegie and the whole of the success literature are marked with the characteristic of single vision. The McGuffey *Readers* sum it up nicely by teaching that we are the architects of our own fortune. The biblical vision of life, of land, of fortune as the gifts of God is missing. Where once stood God, the giver of gifts, now there is a rational understanding of the laws of the universe. The biblical story sees brothers and sisters in covenant in the land. Because life is full of surprises and sufferings, some are rich and some are poor, but all are full participants in the covenant. Thus all are to be gifted by one another even as they have been gifted by God.

But the rational vision of the universe sees no gifts, no contingencies, no surprises, and therefore no requirement for living life in response to gift. While the laws of the universe are understood to have been given by providence, still it is up to us to work out our lives within the framework provided by these laws. If we do what is useful, if we are industrious, frugal, and self-disciplined in both reality and in appearance, we will be successful. The fit survive; the fittest rise to the top—that is the law of the universe. It is in our power to train ourselves to the level of fitness that we truly desire, and therefore truly deserve.

It is not that there is a lack of good gifts or of fortuitous happenings in the lives of Franklin or Carnegie. Much happens to them that persons of twofold vision would see as the gift of God. Franklin finds Meredith in Keimer's shop and they become friends. When Keimer dismisses Franklin after an argument, Meredith hunts up Franklin and proposes that they go into business together with capital from Meredith's father. When Meredith's alcoholism threatens the business, Franklin's friends, on their own initiative, offer to advance enough money to enable Franklin to buy out Meredith's share of the partnership. Although Franklin is grateful, he does not use the occasion to teach a moral nor does he use either incident to think about how one advances in the world. His teaching centers on matters that are not contingent but are within his control. Thus, against his own experience, he argues that we are the architects of our own fortune.

Carnegie also had the gift of a beginning. He once reflected that "upon trifles the best gifts of the gods often hang." The trifle in his case was a conversation between the manager of the telegraph office and his uncle, over a game of checkers. The manager liked to hire boys from his Scottish homeland and wondered if Carnegie's uncle knew a good boy. The uncle did, and Carnegie became a telegraph boy in Pittsburgh. Subsequently the manager of the Western Division of the Pennsylvania Railroad, Thomas Scott, needed an operator for the new railroad telegraph. Scott had regularly used Carnegie's services at the telegraph office and so invited him to join the Pennsylvania as its western operator. As Scott's personal telegraph operator and private secretary, Carnegie quickly learned the elements of railroading. Whenever Scott was promoted, he promoted Carnegie. When good investments came to Scott's attention, he would loan Carnegie a little money to invest. Carnegie's fortune began with a small investment in the Woodruff Sleeping Car Company, an investment that was secured for Carnegie by negotiations between Scott and Theodore Woodruff. The $217.50 investment was soon returning $5000 per year, which was more than triple Carnegie's salary from the railroad. Shortly thereafter Scott became vice president of the Pennsylvania Railroad and promoted Carnegie to his old position as superintendent of the Western Division.

Carnegie, however, soon forgot that the investment was a gift. To him, the story of how he became involved with the Woodruff Sleeping Car Company was an example of his own brilliant business insight, an exercise of the superior ability that enabled the fittest to rise to the top. He liked to tell the story of how he was approached one day on the train by Woodruff, who

> wished me to look at an invention he had made. With that he drew from a green bag . . . a small model of a sleeping berth

for railway cars. He had not spoken a minute, before, like a flash, the whole range of discovery burst upon me. "Yes," I said, "that is something which this continent must have."

. . . Upon my return I laid it before Mr. Scott, declaring that it was one of the inventions of the age. . . . Arrangements were made to build two trial cars, and run them on the Pennsylvania Railroad. I was offered an interest in the venture.[31]

Woodruff remembered the encounter quite differently. In a letter to the *Philadelphia Sunday News* after Carnegie's version of the story was published, Woodruff pointed out that he had already placed twenty-one of his sleeping cars on other railroads before he applied to the Pennsylvania. He recalled that he met with Scott in one of those cars. Scott inspected the car, approved it, and negotiated the contract that established the new company. Scott told Woodruff he wanted to reserve a small share of the company for "a boy in his office." The boy turned out to be Andrew Carnegie.[32]

Needless to say, Carnegie's version of the story received the wider circulation. It served as an example of how by always being ready to attend to business a man could surely become a success. Carnegie saw his life in the way he told the Woodruff story. Although he wrote about how he came to be a telegraph operator and of the role of Scott, he did not reflect upon the gifts involved in these beginnings. Industry, perseverance, frugality, punctuality, reliability, and a passion to learn all that was possible as fast as possible were the virtues that Carnegie taught through his *Autobiography*. Like Franklin, he did not reflect upon gifts he had received nor think about the relation of such gifts and success. Indeed, because of his involvement with the ideas of Darwin and Spencer, Carnegie's world was even more bound to the laws of cause and effect than was the world of Franklin.

The stories that Franklin and Carnegie tell take place within the world of the Enlightenment. Their interpretative framework is the mechanical logic of cause and effect. They point out how a particular outcome necessarily follows upon a particular action. Therefore, those who imitate their virtues will surely imitate their successes. Their stories pass without comment over sufferings or surprises, contingencies or confessions. To be sure, the reader of these autobiographies can see that the action of each writer takes place in an existing web of relationships, in the presence of other persons whose action affects the outcome of the story. But the writers do not emphasize this aspect of their world. The world of which they write is a cosmic machine.

Because they stress the theme of progress, we do not gain much insight into either Franklin or Carnegie as characters. They do not grow, suffer, agonize, love, promise, or forgive. At the end of the story, we know more about them, but we do not know them. We have read another story about the self-made man in America. The role remains the same. The virtues remain the same. The world remains the same. Therefore, if one would walk in their footsteps, one must practice the virtue of hard work and success will follow. To live in such a world and to understand one's life in such a way is to be a person of single vision. It is to have a master image of the self.

When we read the autobiographies, however, we cannot help but notice that both writers persistently avoid spelling out one aspect of their relationship to the world even when it would be appropriate so to do. This aspect is, of course, the gifts that come their way and the meaning of those gifts, or better, the meaning of life that is lived in the presence of such contingencies and surprises. It is evident from their early lives that both Franklin and Carnegie have the gift of unusual intelligence and are deeply indebted to mentors and friends for their early good fortune.

Carnegie's real story differs even more markedly from his cover story than Franklin's version of his life differs from reality. Carnegie's life story is more truly represented as that of a person who lives out his life within the game of "corporation." Carnegie was rich early in life; afterward he had no need to be involved in business, much less in the cutthroat sort of business he pursued: driving competitors bankrupt, hiring an army of Pinkerton guards to destroy the union at the Homestead plant, and dismissing fifteen partners for not pursuing profit avidly enough. But work had become a game whose endlessly fascinating moves had captured and dominated him. The traditional understandings of work as either a necessity or a godly calling no longer applied to Carnegie. In a real sense, Carnegie's ethic is the ethic of winning. The story of success, of the survival of the fittest, serves as its cover story.

The story of success preserves the identity of the successful person at the cost of failing to account for any other relationships, other aspects of reality. This self-deception is a result of the kind of story told about self and world. The story of success has few resources to combat self-deception. It does not give a person the skills to recognize the relationship between the real story and the cover story. There is little ground on which to re-examine one's life. There is only success or self-condemnation for failing to develop the character that would ensure the achievements that the story of success requires. That achievement consists, of course, in reaching the top. This story affirms again and again that there is plenty of room at the top. Failure to reach it is personal moral failure.

The story of failure is the flip side of the story of success. Poverty is considered to be good if it was the soil from which the successful person sprang. Both Franklin and Carnegie, like most writers of the success literature of the nineteenth century, point out that the successful person often begins in poverty. But to end in poverty is quite a different matter. While want and need are inevitable, the gospel of success attributes their cause to the character of the person who suffers them, not to God, as did Winthrop, or to the social situation, as did later reformers. Indigence is the punishment the universe metes out to the person of poor character, who will not train himself or herself in the virtues of industry and efficiency.

The steady attack on the character of the poor also served to fuel the racism directed against blacks, native Americans, and Mexican Americans. Those groups that suffered from discrimination also suffered the most from poverty. To racists, poverty was but a further sign of the degradation of despised groups.

Conclusion

Stories enable us to see the world in a new way. If the story is true, it is heuristic: that is, it enables us to go on asking questions, to think with the freshness that precedes discovery. As we begin to evaluate the story of success, we need to inquire into both the truth and the power of the story. It is clear that it is powerful. It has endured for centuries and shaped the character of many persons.

The story has power because, first of all, it is rooted in the Enlightenment framework of the story of progress. In the story of progress, the whole creation is rising to a higher plane through the mechanism of natural selection. The story of success borrows the language and images of cause and effect, of mechanistic action. Therefore it offers clear, straightforward explanations. Life can be controlled, and, more to the point, the story promises me that I can control my own life. I can exercise the virtue of hard work, and hard work is sure to bring success. Because hard work and success are related in some situations, the story of success seems to be confirmed as an image of self and world. Its explanations and promise of control are attractive in a world that appears all too often to be subject to all sorts of contingencies and contradictions and sufferings.

But the story of success does not enable us to go on asking questions, to think with freshness about the whole web of relationships in which human action takes place. We not only act but are acted upon. Our deeds and sufferings take place within a world characterized by contingency, contradictions, and limits. The story of success denies the mystery of human life. It does not take account of those surprises, either gifts or sufferings, that surround human action.

Second, it overlooks the reality of the limits of the world of the vast majority of persons. The iron cage of poverty in which millions live out their lives is not unlocked by the declaration that hard work equals success. The story of success is destructive for all those who have been dispossessed in America. In contrast to the biblical story, the story of success divides us rather than binds us together. Instead of seeing the poor, the stranger, the wayfarer, the widow, and the orphan as brothers and sisters, the story of success sees them as persons who have failed. It argues that failure is deserved, for each person may succeed if only he or she will make the effort to develop the good character that is required. Therefore the story of success sees the dispossessed as persons of poor character who have gotten what they deserve. Such a perspective encourages self-righteousness and discourages compassion and care.

The story of success is destructive even to those who succeed and who account themselves worthwhile. They no longer live in human community where persons are encouraged to discover the resources to love one another. There is in this story no sense of living together in covenant with the God who cares for the oppressed and therefore bids us care for the oppressed.

Third, the story of success provides no resources for the struggle against self-deception. Both Franklin and Carnegie overlook the fact that they are given many great gifts. Franklin's story is easier to appreciate and perhaps learn from because of his self-deprecating humor and his constant use of irony. Nonetheless, those actions that he believes mark the development of his character are clearly only partially responsible for his success. Since Carnegie lacks the redeeming grace of ironic humor, his story is much more difficult to believe. So both stories seem to be cover stories. The real story has to do with being providentially placed within a world with fewer limits than most, with being given gifts that are wholly undeserved, and finally with a disciplined and skillful response to those gifts.

Although the story of success captured the imagination of many Americans and became a dominant theme in much of the popular literature of the late nineteenth century, its denial of community and its false reading of the limits of the real world of the industrial revolution raised up movements to oppose its perspective. It is significant that the movements that opposed those who preached the gospel of success proclaimed in one form or another a gospel in which all persons are bound together as brothers and sisters in one human family. The people of the social gospel movement, or the labor movement, or the Grange, thought that daily life shows the need to exercise compassion one for the other and the necessity of finding resources for responding more adequately to the crises of the age. Later in the twentieth century, figures such as César Chavez and Martin Luther King, Jr., recovered many of the resources of the biblical story for the poor and despised in America. Yet as the century nears its end, it is clear that the story of success in America still serves as an interpretative framework for many persons of the rising middle class.

4

The Story of Well-being

In the 1980s, the story of well-being occupies a central place as the dominant cultural narrative in America. The primary image of self and world is no longer that of faithfulness to the covenant, or of the hardworking self-discipline that gains the heights of economic success. In the present ethos, people seek to be faithful to the true inner self, and success is imagined in terms of developing a sense of wellbeing.

The transformation of the American sense of self and world was neither sudden nor complete. The psychological image of well-being emerged from the cultural turmoil of the late nineteenth century and represented Americans' attempt to reconstruct a coherent sense of identity in a time when earlier images of self seemed to be disintegrating. As T. J. Jackson Lears has argued, the perception of self underwent a number of major changes. First, persons who were migrating to urban areas began to develop a sense of personal anonymity. For the emerging middle class, the community of neighbors who fashioned a self through the shared reality of daily work had disappeared. A person could no longer be observed pushing a wheelbarrow full of paper through the streets in the early morning. The world of face-to-face community had passed. Anonymity was the new reality to which all new city dwellers were required to respond.[1]

Second, this change in the character of work had a significant impact on the image of the self. Selfhood had previously been shaped by the reality of physical work. Henry Thoreau, in his well-known essay *Walden*, had shown how hoeing beans could be used to discipline the self into the deliberate life.[2] Likewise, to grow food, bake bread, make soup, or set type in the community of others who were going about the same tasks was to discipline the self, which in turn brought the sure reward of both economic and moral progress. But as bureaucratic tasks replaced physical work for the middle class, older ideas of selfhood became more and more difficult to sustain. The conviction grew that hard physical work no longer had the potency to shape one's character or success.

Third, what Alan Trachtenberg has referred to as the "incorporation of America" meant the emergence of a changed, more tightly structured society with vast new hierarchies of control. A decreasing number of corporations exercised control over an ever-increasing share of American industry. The lifework of more and more persons was directed by an elite, interlocking system of corporate boards. The successful entrepreneurs who gained large fortunes in the nineteenth century had become an elite ruling class that dominated the industrial world of the twentieth century. In such a corporate, bureaucratic world, most persons no longer imagined success in terms of entrepreneurs like Carnegie. They hoped for the more modest goal of a move to the middle-class world of managers; instead of a swift rise from rags to riches, they hoped to climb the rungs of management.[3]

In the figurative sense, then, the incorporation of America meant a change in the representative character of the age—from entrepreneur to manager. A representative character is a certain type of social role that embodies the dominant moral beliefs of a society and powerfully shapes the moral and personal traits of those who take up those roles. This change in representative characters therefore signaled a change in the dominant perspective. Personality was much more important for a manager than for an entrepreneur, for managers were required to deal with other personalities and interpersonal responses as they sought to persuade, inspire, and manipulate people to meet the goals of their organizations.[4]

Fourth, a good personality soon came to mean more than the key to advancement. With a good personality one could feel good about oneself in a circle of personal friends without regard to the more public achievement of success. Development of one's own well-being came to be perceived as the best response to anonymity and the change in the character of work.[5]

Fifth, liberal Protestantism assimilated the biblical story into the modern creed of progress by making faith depend on the explanatory power of reason. But a faith that depended so much on reason was attacked from within by a new kind of doubt. Late Victorians, who lived in what they called "modern doubt," questioned all things, but they were especially skeptical of the ability of reason to answer the question of the existence of God. The biblical story had provided a distinct vision of the self and a framework of meaning for life. But when the existence of God was called into question, the biblical framework decayed, and a new vision of self appeared. A person might choose to aid a neighbor who had been beaten and robbed on the way from Jerusalem to Jericho, but the choice would not be made on the basis of faithfulness to the covenant but on whether one might feel better about oneself.[6]

In the twentieth century, then, the way we envision ourselves is different from either the success or biblical stories. In the cultural narrative of well-being, we seek self-realization, self-worth, and self-esteem. We wish to be attractive, charismatic, creative, dominant, or forceful. But we think not only about self but about our world with these images, which arise from psychotherapy. The therapeutic attitude enters the world of work and helps us translate our experience of a bureaucratic society into personal meanings. When we speak of our marriages, families, friends, communities, and society we talk in terms of communication, empathy, authenticity, and well-being. Although most persons do not participate in therapy, still the therapeutic metaphors have become a major resource for thinking about society as well as about self. Thus, along with the manager, there is a second representative character, that of the therapist.

Therefore, if we are to understand the story twentieth-century American culture is telling, the story of well-being, we need to examine the web of connections that binds together the two representative characters of our age—the therapist and the manager—and the consumer society that sustains them. We will examine aspects of the consumer society, such as mass marketing, mass entertainment, therapeutic religion, and character of personal relationships.[7]

The Rise of Psychotherapy

From the perspective of the psychoanalytic movement, the science of psychoanalysis was a continuation of the Enlightenment story of progress. Even though the leading intellectual of the movement, Sigmund Freud, understood his psychology as a new sort of self-consciousness, he believed still that his claims concerning the character of the human condition were grounded in scientific reason. In spite of the fact that he took his clues from what seems to be the most subjective of human constructions, the inner workings of the individual mind, Freud believed that the theory he constructed from these clues articulated the universal, objective truth concerning the structure of the psyche.

From the perspective of James Hillman, however, Freud's genius is not his continuation of the logic of the Enlightenment. Freud's genius appears in his invention of a new literary genre, the case history, as the vehicle to carry his psychoanalytic vision into the world. His psychoanalytic case histories are a new way of plotting human experience. The plot tells us the "why" of the action. Every Freudian narrative, although thick with intense complications of transference and resistance, displays the same answer to the question, Why? Freud answers the question with literary flair. His case histories are written in the style of a detective story. A mystery is unfolding. The mystery is repression, which is followed by passions and miseries (symptom formation), the involvement of the therapist (transference), and the lifting of the repression through the practice of the analytic attitude.[8]

For Freud, however, the analytic attitude is not a cure but a lifelong task that each individual person must take up. The task is taken up in the spirit of a scientist, with the self as the ultimate object of the new science. A person carefully examines all the options that promise to enhance or organize his or her life. Life is subject to such painful ambiguities that well-being is rightfully recognized as a rare and fine personal achievement.[9]

Freud believes that well-being is such an achievement because there is no natural harmony or order of values universally recognized and taken up by the human community. Human nature is not structured according to a natural hierarchy of high and low or good and evil. Each person is an egalitarian mob of conflicting dispositions. Human beings are creatures who at once love and hate, desire to succeed and want to fail, wish to lead and yearn to be led. Freud in the end characterizes human nature as the locus of the eternal conflict between Eros, the life instinct, and Thanatos, the death instinct.

Since the urbanization of Western culture eroded the supportive, face-to-face community, Freud introduced psychoanalysis as a way through the loneliness of competitive modern culture and around the question of meaning. Psychoanalysis taught the individual how to nurture his or her own sense of well-being in the midst of the scramble for the survival of the fittest. According to Philip Rieff, Freud established a new ideal image of selfhood: a person who has an analytic attitude, something of a genius about self, and no dependence upon any community; a person who is an integrated personality in a disintegrating society, a sane self in a mad world; a person who cannot conceive of an action that is not self-serving, the healthy hypochondriac who knows how to live with no higher purpose than a durable sense of well-being.[10]

It is the analytic attitude that enables the individual to understand and then to tolerate such ambiguities. The power of insight gives a wider range of choice. The mature person, Freud thinks, has learned that life's true task is to discover how to reduce one's own suffering by reducing the demands one makes upon oneself in the major situations of life: love and work, friendship and citizenship. Each of us must learn how to live with the contradictions that make us the person we are, and thus recognize that while we cannot re-create either self or world, we are able to learn the art of being kinder to the self. In the midst of conflicting passions, Freud hopes that insight will enable reason to reassert itself quietly and unobtrusively; i.e., that the choices persons make will be reasonable choices. But Freud does not instruct his patients or his readers whether one choice is the better choice. Freud's concern is to enable persons to do less harm than they might otherwise do, and to increase their personal capacity to choose.

Philip Rieff contrasts Freud's interest in the analytic attitude with the cultural interest in discovering a cure for the ills that beset us. Freud does not speak of curing a patient, because he believes that to cure a person means to commit that person to a particular vision of the good. Such work is the task of a religious community, and Freud sets the analytic attitude against all such subordination of the individual to the community. Although Freud believes his patients can be set free to make their own choices, he does not believe that the content of one choice is to be recommended as truer than another.[11]

Jung criticizes Freud for shaping all life stories to one psychoanalytic plot. Jung's plotting, his theory of archetypes, is inherently multiplistic and gives more weight to individual character than to the necessity of plot. Jung develops his plots in the awareness that persons in Western culture yearn to be cured of anxiety. To be cured is to find the assurance that our choices are authentic, that our lives are meaningful. Rieff points out that Jung's theory of archetypes and his technique of dream analysis make it possible for each patient to discover the character of the eternal order or god within. Each individual replots his or her personal story in terms of obedience to the inner god.

Obedience sets one free from both the painful ambiguities of life and the endless task of the analytic attitude.[12]

Since, according to Jung, sickness is a form of misunderstanding, once a person understands the character of his or her individual god within, he or she can choose to pattern life accordingly. This inner religion requires that each person examine his or her own myth—not to determine whether it is good or evil, true or false—but to discover how to live in harmony with that myth and so increase our own sense of well-being. Jung thus provides a language of faith that serves the individual without requiring the individual to live in the covenanted community. By examining his or her own dreams and fantasies, each individual integrates personal symbols into the common symbolic universe of the archetypes, and so "gains membership in the invisible church of common meanings." This strictly personal faith is a form of edifying self-examination. It enhances well-being by distracting the individual from the anxiety of inauthenticity and the fear of the meaninglessness of living.[13]

Freud and Jung were first popularized in America in the period of the mind-power movement and progressivism, both of which were passionately committed to the belief that human beings could improve themselves and their environment. For these movements, it was this power of self-improvement that restored human beings to a position of preeminence in the cosmic order of things, and thus bestowed a fundamental meaning on human life.

The Progressive movement sought to bring sorely needed reforms to a society suffering the injustices and class conflicts of early industrial America. The Progressives were convinced that the reforms would enable the oppressed to improve themselves. The desired reforms were to be achieved by rejecting politics itself in favor of a manager-oriented society—a government of efficient experts who understood psychology and social science, and who could thus make the system work.[14]

For those in the mind-power movement, however, reform of the world began with the renewal of the individual. The movement claimed to teach persons how to heal their bodies and control their lives through the practice of mental health. By the onset of the twentieth century, the movement was concentrating on the enhancement of the ego and the cultivation of personal power and self-mastery. Mind-power advocates believed that control of thought brought not only physical healing, as in the Gospel stories, but also ensured happiness and success.

Freud criticized and thoroughly distrusted the style of the American advocates of self-fulfillment. Freud sought to make his lessons difficult, but his American popularizers also saw the self, improved, as the ultimate concern of a culture in the midst of fundamental change. To Freud's chagrin, the message of the popularizers—that well-being provided the best answer to the perennial questions concerning the meaning of life—was readily accepted in America.

The cultural movement that sought well-being through self-mastery received further encouragement with the emergence of the behaviorist school of psychology in the 1920s. In his classic book *Behaviorism,* John B. Watson provided scientific grounding for the faith of mind-power advocates by arguing that human beings were able to transform themselves and their environment. Watson's vision was taken up by the popularizers of psychology, who urged persons to practice certain psychological techniques, such as repeated affirmations, in order to draw upon the power of the subconscious. Émile Coué, one of the better-known popularizers, taught persons to recite, "Day by day, in every way, I am getting better and better." An increasing number of Americans embraced the view that human beings could refashion themselves, increase their sense of well-being, and thus live happier and more meaningful lives by the proper use of the new science.[15]

Although psychoanalysis provides the intellectual foundation for the new perspective on self and world, the practice of therapy itself has a continuing impact on the culture. As a practice, the therapeutic relationship is a model for many modern relationships. The therapeutic relationship is one in which there is deep emotional bonding, a closeness between persons, and an honesty of communication. The relationship is also carefully circumscribed, emotionally distanced, and asymmetrical. One person does most of the talking. The other person does most of the listening. These features establish therapy as a relationship that has a definite purpose: the development of the patient's sense of well-being.[16]

As the therapeutic relationship seeks a psychologically effective way to create a sense of well-being, so in managerial and professional life persons relate to others briefly, specifically, and intensely. As Bellah points out, much of what managers and professionals do is communicate. To be economically effective, a manager often needs to be "factually accurate, emotionally attuned, and intersubjectively subtle." The demanding interactions of managerial or professional careers require the communicative skills of the therapist. Thus a whole subdiscipline of therapy has come into being in which the therapist has exchanged the task of teaching marriage partners how to communicate for the challenge of teaching managers how to communicate. Such a development underlines the importance of therapy as a model for managers.[17]

Well-being in the Consumer Society

Because the representative characters of therapist and manager embody the dominant moral beliefs of consumer society, they maintain a consumer culture and are in turn sustained by it. The marks of consumer society appear in other arenas as well. We shall examine four of them: mass marketing, mass entertainment, therapeutic religion, and personal relationships.

Mass Marketing

Managers are interested in communicating not only to individuals but also to large audiences of consumers. This form of communication has been institutionalized in national mass marketing. As we noted earlier, the story of well-being is the story being told by the American culture in the twentieth century. National mass marketing is a twentieth-century institution that serves an important role in the telling of the new American vision of self.[18]

T. J. Jackson Lears has traced the relationship between advertising strategies and the therapeutic ethos. By the turn of the century, advertisers began to do more than simply attract attention to the product and present information to the consumer. Albert Lasker and Claude Hopkins in Chicago developed the "reason why" approach to advertising. The reason given for the purchase of the product was not related to its practical use; instead, the message appealed to the desires of the consumer by showing how the product would provide the purchaser with a richer, fuller life.[19]

Therapeutic advertising became institutionalized as major firms hired psychological consultants such as John B. Watson. Watson's views that human behavior could be manipulated convinced advertisers that therapeutic advertising could be a method of social control. Consumer demand for particular products could be aroused by associating the products with imaginary states of well-being in social life, family life, business success, and patriotism. A dazzling smile, fresh breath, an alluring aura, or sparkling floors opened doors to romantic experiences, professional advancement, and social acceptance.

Even the mission of America was reinterpreted by the advertisers. In the midst of World War II, Hoover Vacuum Cleaner Company ads transformed Norman Rockwell's mythic American villagers into patriotic American consumers. In a *Saturday Evening Post* advertisement, an old woman, a middle-aged man, and a young girl clutch neatly bound packages in their arms. Their upturned Rockwell faces meet a shaft of providential sunlight. Three years after Roosevelt's speech proclaiming that the purpose of the war was to establish the "Four Freedoms"—freedom of religion and speech, freedom from want and fear—the Hoover ad proclaims that the "Fifth Freedom Is Freedom of Choice." The slogan was an apt summary of the perspective of the advertising industry. The war itself was placed in the context of the therapeutic ethos. The *Saturday Evening Post* ad suggests that the ready availability of consumer goods had become as crucial to the well-being of Americans as were freedom of religion and speech and freedom from want and fear.[20]

Advertisers were well aware that women also yearned for a more fulfilling life. Therefore the trade journals stressed the importance of reaching women and argued that women were especially vulnerable to emotional appeals. Advertisers capitalized upon the feminist movement, offering women the freedom they desired through consumption—smoking Lucky Strikes, buying "natural" underwear, or living freely every day of their lives thanks to Kotex.

By the late 1920s, the symbolic universe of national advertising was nearly indistinguishable from the therapeutic ethos. This worldview was congenial to the interests of managers in that it created consumer demand for their products. Therapy was a resource for managers as they sought to manipulate consumers as well as employees. It is clear that the possibility of managing and marketing in the modern sense required the sense of self and world in which there is "nothing at stake beyond a manipulatable sense of well-being."[21]

Mass Entertainment

The new form of mass entertainment, the motion picture, also became an important part of the therapeutic ethos. The motion picture industry's new "star" system emphasized personality. Although the star played different roles in various movies, the basic on-screen personality remained the same, an expression of youthful vitality that overcame the ordinariness of the everyday and promised a life of fulfillment. The fulfillment promised was usually sexual and financial.

Douglas Fairbanks incarnated the connections among advertising, motion pictures, and the therapeutic ethos. He not only became one of the first stars to endorse products for pay, but he also played characters who demonstrated the new path to fulfillment. In *His Picture in the Papers,* Fairbanks created the role of a young man who worked in the office of Pringle Products, the cereal company his father founded. The dull father, who was both a vegetarian and teetotaler, required that his son follow the same path of plain living, hard work, and duty. But the son, a vibrant personality, concealed a martini mix in his lunch bag, learned to box, became attractive to "new women," and at last rescued a big businessman from criminals. As his picture was being taken for the papers, reporters asked where he found the energy to do so much. The son answered, "Pringle Products!" Sales of Pringle Products soon skyrocketed, for they were now seen as creators of robust fun lovers rather than boring vegetarians. The film, like the rest of Fairbanks's career, made it clear that having a positive, vibrant personality had become the royal road to success and well-being.[22]

Therapeutic Religion

The spread of the therapeutic ethos was enhanced by the common vision shared by many different sectors of the culture. The development of therapeutic religion was especially important. The religious affirmation of the search for well-being confirmed the moral seriousness of such a quest and inspired many to undertake the task. We can understand the development of the main themes of therapeutic religion and its connection to other sectors in the culture by briefly examining four of the major figures in therapeutic religion from the 1920s to the 1980s: Bruce Barton, Harry Emerson Fosdick, Norman Vincent Peale, and Robert Schuller.

In the 1920s Bruce Barton became an outstanding example of the connections between advertising and therapeutic religion. Barton was a founder of a major advertising firm, a successful magazine journalist, and an author. His books stressed the possibilities open to those with positive attitudes and healthy personalities.[23]

Barton's best-seller was *The Man Nobody Knows* (1924), in which Jesus appeared as a healthy personality, with physical strength, bounding pulse, hot desires, and perfect teeth. His message bubbled with the optimism of the search for self-realization and met the widespread longings for a "more abundant life." The "steel like hardness of his nerves" and his "consuming sincerity" enabled him to become the most successful advertising man in history. Jesus willingly placed himself center stage with a dramatic healing or a raging controversy in order to promote his message. The language of the parables—simple, condensed, repetitive, sincere—was a model for advertising copy. His creed did not deny life, but enhanced it, and his righteousness was a righteousness that led to a "happier, more satisfying way of living." Barton's Jesus was the full joining of advertising ideology to therapeutic ideals and religious experience.[24]

Because of his religious interests, Barton developed a moral justification for advertising. His advertising copy assumed that the products contributed to the betterment of human life, the progress of the individual, and the improvement of the nation. Thus in one General Electric ad he proclaimed: "Any woman who is doing any household task that a little electric motor can do is working for three cents an hour. Human life is too precious to be sold at the price of three cents an hour."[25]

Barton also believed that the new techniques of mass communication could remake the social order. Although he recognized that the cruelties of competition and dishonesty continued to stain much of business, the optimism that informed his approach to religion also enabled him to believe that advertising was gradually reforming business. In his "Creed of an Advertising Man," he proclaimed that advertising was a moral good because advertising compelled business to set up public ideals of quality and service and measure up to those ideals. In addition to generating jobs that have expanded the economy and given us the highest standard of living in the world, advertising is "essential to the continuance of the democratic process.

Advertising sustains a system that has made us leaders of the free world."[26]

Barton's moral justification of advertising was plausible because the search for well-being was becoming an important aspect of the American religious scene. Indeed, therapeutic religion became one of the fundamental creators of the milieu in which Barton's advertising ethos could flourish. Nearly 60 percent of Americans counted themselves as members of a church or synagogue, and over 40 percent reported attending a religious service at least once a month. Since by the 1930s many of the best-known religious leaders were already translating the biblical story into the therapeutic idiom, Barton's point of view was readily accepted.

Harry Emerson Fosdick, the most influential liberal preacher in the 1930s and 1940s, understood himself as a proclaimer of a therapeutic Christianity in both personal and social arenas. In his book *Adventurous Religion,* Fosdick demanded that every religious custom and doctrine pass two tests: "First, is it intelligently defensible; second, does it contribute to man's abundant life?" Underlying this ethos was a conviction that self-realization was the fundamental purpose of human existence. Fosdick argues that "religion's central and unique property is power to release faith and courage for living, to produce spiritual vitality and fruitfulness; and by that it ultimately stands or falls." This was no new nor passing vision for Fosdick. The persons he used as examples of true religion in book after book and sermon after sermon were persons who won through great difficulties a more abundant life.[27]

Fosdick's heroes, however, did not find a simple peace. His preaching was not full of the bubbly optimism of the mind-power movement. No, for Fosdick peace was fundamentally a matter of power. Religious persons had that interior resource of power, that margin of reserve, that sent them into each day's tasks and difficulties "sure that what they ought to do they can do and what they must endure they can stand."[28] Religion was a support in time of suffering and a call to strenuous effort in time of a neighbor's need, for faith in someone or something tapped unused reserves of power.

Although Fosdick recognized that religion gave persons the power to do what they ought to do, most of his suggestions concerning what persons ought to do returned the power of religion to the familiar arena of self. "A real person achieves a high degree of unity within himself. He does not remain split and scattered but gets himself together into wholeness and coherence. . . . All other tests of success in personal living hark back to this—a real person is integrated."[29] If a person was already integrated and found himself or herself quite at peace with and comfortable in the world, Fosdick would not presume, as did Jonathan Edwards or Franklin, to tell that person what to do to live a *good* life. His interest was not salvation or character, but well-being. As Donald Meyer has pointed out, this longing for psychic well-being as an end in itself, rather than as one outcome of religious faith, was new to the history of Western Christianity.[30]

By mid-century it often seemed as if religion had no other purpose than to meet the longing for psychic well-being. *The Power of Positive Thinking,* by Norman Vincent Peale, was a best-seller throughout the 1950s. Only the Bible topped it in sales in the nonfiction category. Peale assured his readers that his new techniques would enable them to gain control over their lives. The person who practiced positive thinking had the opportunity to become an esteemed and well-liked person, attain health and influence, and enjoy a delightful new sense of well-being.[31]

Peale's techniques turn out to be the two basic techniques of the mind-power movement. First, he urges his readers to "use one of the most powerful laws in this world, a law recognized alike by psychology and religion, namely, change your mental habits to belief instead of disbelief." Peale believes that persons can alter their attitudes by stamping on their minds a mental picture of themselves as succeeding. Whenever a negative thought comes to mind, a person must deliberately voice a positive thought to cancel it out. This focusing of consciousness is the first step in establishing an inner sense of well-being.

The second technique that Peale recommends is the practice of repeated affirmations. "Ten times each day practice the following affirmation . . . I can do all things through Christ who strengthens me." He recommends the practice of faith by saying "I believe" the first thing every morning before getting out of bed. He tells story after story of how persons turned from abject failures into glowing successes through choosing positive thinking and the practice of repeated affirmations.[32]

Even though in his stress on success Peale shares some common ground with Franklin, Peale still presents a fundamentally different perspective. Peale does not speak of the virtues that the community will recognize and reward—hard work, honesty, frugality, good craftsmanship, or citizenship. His vision is radically individual. Well-being is a matter of training the mind. Mind training is able to "regenerate a person, bring him into touch with his own creative forces, and in turn, with the infinite forces of the universe." Peale agrees with Jung that the real relationships that require our attention are those within our own minds, "our creative forces" and those that are universal, the archetypes, or the "infinite forces of the universe." The particular, local, flesh-and-blood community in which the individual lives is no longer a central concern of Peale and those who teach the way to well-being.[33]

The explosive growth of the audience for the electronic church in the 1970s and 1980s is dramatic evidence that the face-to-face community is no longer a central concern for many Americans. Those whose church appears only on the television screen believe that real religion has to do with the creative forces of the mind. The best example of the spread of therapeutic religion via the electronic church is Peale's most visible protégé and successor, Robert H. Schuller. Schuller's readers are reminded that he is "pastor of the world-famous Crystal Cathedral. . . . No minister or priest or rabbi speaks to more people every week in the world [on the television program *The Hour of Power*]."[34]

Schuller argues for the power of "possibility thinking." Possibility thinking is the secret that enables people to view their problems in such a way that they become winners rather than losers. Winners accept that everyone has problems, that every problem has a limited life span, and that the key is to understand that problems hold positive possibilities. Winners believe they can discover and respond to these positive possibilities. Although Schuller uses examples of persons who succeed in business through possibility thinking, his primary emphasis is on achieving a durable sense of well-being.[35]

In a series of lectures to the faculty and student body of Western Theological Seminary, Schuller points out that "self-esteem is the single greatest need facing the human race today" and argues that the religion of Jesus can best meet that need when it is wholly translated into the therapeutic idiom. His use of the Lord's Prayer provides a good example of what such a translation achieves.[36]

According to Schuller, the Lord's Prayer is Christ's solution to the problems caused by the six basic negative emotions: inferiority, depression, anxiety, guilt, resentment, and fear. Inferiority is overcome by recognizing that God is Father, and that we are all part of God's family and therefore all of value; depression is replaced with hope as we pray for God's kingdom to come; anxiety is replaced by security in the prayer for daily bread. But what if we have some great task and find that we don't have what it takes? "Is success important? Yes, it is terribly important. For nothing is more destructive to a person's self-esteem than the fear of being a terrible failure!" So we must trust God to handle our anxiety over success and failure. Guilt is set aside as we pray, "Forgive us our trespasses." In turn, our own self-esteem is protected as we forgive others. The closing petition, "Lead us not into temptation but deliver us from evil," sustains self-esteem by dealing a death blow to fear. In his prayer, therefore, Jesus is teaching us how to replace "self-esteem-strangulating, negative emotions with positive, health-generating emotions."[37]

Schuller's teachings reach beyond the confines of the Crystal Cathedral and *The Hour of Power*. He lectures from coast to coast to many professional and corporate audiences. Since the days of Bruce Barton, perhaps no one has spoken so widely to both the worlds of business and church. Schuller applies his understanding of possibility thinking to the perennial question of managers: "How shall we successfully motivate persons and manage our enterprises?" In accord with the general movement of the culture, Schuller turns to the therapist for resources with which to instruct the manager.

In all his work, Schuller develops the themes of therapeutic religion. The biblical images of covenant and cross are transformed by the image of well-being. The way of the kingdom of God, the way of discipleship, is no longer a narrow way. The way of the cross is translated into a way of overcoming negative emotions. In Schuller and the electronic church the religious search for psychic well-being has become common coin in American society.

Personal Relationships

The intense search for well-being appears not only in public segments of society such as advertising, mass entertainment, and the electronic church, but also within the personal relationships that are central to the way life is experienced in every culture. In *The Culture of Narcissism*, Christopher Lasch suggests that in contemporary America people demand from personal relations a richness and intensity that previously had been reserved for religious experience. Although in some ways the demands men and women make upon one another have been lessened, in other ways the demands have increased. The fundamental change is the requirement that each relationship be evaluated in terms of its power to develop a person's own sense of well-being. If a relationship does not serve the purpose of enhancing one's sense of well-being, it is to be terminated.[38]

The placing of such heavy demands on personal relationships increases their emotional risks. Lasch argues that although men and women today appear to invest personal relationships with enormous emotional importance, the appearance is an illusion. The intense interest in one's own well-being leads to the cultivation of a protective shallowness, an emotional detachment that soon becomes habitual. For instance, some therapeutic authorities urge their clients to express their needs and wishes without reserve—since all needs and wishes have equal legitimacy—but warn them not to expect a single mate to satisfy them. Such advice seeks to meet emotional tensions by reducing the demands men and women make on one another, rather than enabling them to discover ways to meet the demands.[39]

Open Marriage, by Nena and George O'Neill, provides an excellent example of the therapeutic understanding of love and marriage. The O'Neills define open marriage as an honest and open relationship between two people, which includes a commitment to the right of each to grow as an individual. Meaning in marriage must be created by the partners themselves. Each man and woman must find their own reasons for being together. In open marriage, the reason for being together is the discovery and development of one's own well-being, rather than any sense of obligation. Freedom from obligation makes genuine equality possible. Each mate is to be free to pursue the pleasures he or she wishes, so that the open marriage can develop strong individual identities.[40]

Trust is the linchpin of open marriage. "Without trust, open marriage cannot function. Trust is the pivot upon which the open relationship turns." This trust, however, must be an "open" trust, which the O'Neills contrast to the static trust based upon the sense of obligation that still persists in the traditional marriage.

The O'Neills carefully define trust because the meaning of trust depends upon one's sense of self and world. Covenant trust is a trust rooted in the awareness of the grace of God, and in a faithful response to that grace. In the world of progress, trust arises out of an understanding of the mate's character and the expectation that the mate's character and actions will be dependable. Open trust is therapeutic trust. Open trust means "believing in your mate's ability and willingness to cherish and respect your honesty and your open communications . . . trust is the feeling that no matter what you do or say you are not going to be criticized." In the therapeutic world, trust has to do with sharing immediate desires and living for now. Trust is freedom, "the freedom to assume responsibility for your own self first and then to share that human self in love with your partner in a marriage that places no restrictions upon growth, or limits on fulfillment."[41]

The O'Neills clearly spell out their understanding of trust and their reason for marriage in their rationale for extramarital sexual experiences. Since sex is "a natural function that should be enjoyed for its own earthy self without hypocrisy," sexual intercourse is not to be limited to the marital partner. Instead, marriage partners should develop themselves until they are ready to have an extramarital affair that will be rewarding and beneficial to the marriage. But the extramarital affair will be beneficial only if it increases the sense of well-being of both the marriage partners. Since affairs usually lead to jealousy and jealousy to conflict, and since conflict reduces the well-being of both partners, the advice to "develop themselves," then, means that the partners must learn to control jealousy.

Jealousy, however, arises out of intimacy, and intimacy requires the willingness to give of oneself, to place oneself in the hands of the other, to be open to hurt. As Stanley Hauerwas points out, the O'Neills' argument requires that we become persons who are incapable of creating and sustaining intimate relationships. But since both marriage and friendship, traditionally understood, require a giving of the self that opens one to suffering and sorrow as well as joy and celebration, the O'Neills quite logically reject relationships that entail such obligations. Thus their ideas exemplify the way stress on well-being leads to the cultivation of a protective detachment.[42]

The Power and Self-deception in the Story of Well-being

Like the story of success with its concern for character, the story of well-being with its concern for personality has displayed great staying power in our culture. Most of us who live in American culture notice that the old stories, such as the religious stories or the success stories, have been recast in terms of well-being. The story of well-being has such power because it is a response to the history of human life in the modern industrialized world. Much of life is routinized, bureaucratized, and seemingly devoid of the possibility of being affected by the action of the individual. Therefore, the human need to create and fashion a world is focused on the arena in which the individual can participate, the arena of the self.

Like the story of success, the story of well-being fails to account for the whole web of relationships in which human action takes place. Human life has always been lived in a world characterized by contingency, contradiction, and suffering. Suffering is not so much to be overcome as it is to be taken up as part of life lived within community. Vital religious communities share a rich symbolic life that directs the self outward toward communal purposes. Only in such communities can the self be realized and satisfied. Such communities are compassionate, and they share the human condition of suffering, precisely because at their best they interpret personal experiences in the light of community understandings. Suffering is also part of the gift of life. The question is not how to avoid, justify, or eliminate suffering, but how to respond appropriately to it. The story of well-being, however, focuses on a personal technology of the inner life that promises to teach its adherents how to live and not suffer.

The therapeutic ethic is, then, a richly woven cover story that tells of a cure from the pain attendant upon living. Within the story each person is given the power to fashion his or her own cure if only she or he is serious enough and works hard enough at the task. Personal well-being is therefore like economic success in that it is not an achievement to be taken lightly. The disorder that attends life is understood to be such a serious threat because the world is experienced as chaotic. There seems to be no natural order of values nor harmony of nature to guide choice. Therefore, the therapeutic authorities do not search for truth, because there is no truthful order. Instead, they take up whatever story will enhance well-being. So Freud recasts our inner conflicts in terms of the ancient myths, Jung tells stories of inner gods, of a host of inner characters, the archetypes. The advertisers and filmmakers create and capitalize on celebrities and their endorsement of well-being through consumerism, and Barton discovers that Jesus was after all the world's great founder of the advertising business. Schuller is certain that Jesus was not the first great advertiser but the first great psychologist, and the O'Neills retell the story of marriage and translate trust from the language of covenant or character to the freedom to share immediate desires and live for the moment.

The focus on well-being disengages the therapeutic from the search for truth, and thus the story of well-being differs radically from earlier stories. The gospel of success is rooted in the story of progress. Since the universe is law-governed, the truth is out there in the facts. The appropriate response to such a law-governed vision of the world is to discover what facts impinge most nearly upon daily life and respond to them. The most obvious fact is the truth that self-discipline and hard work lead to success. Therefore the way to good character and wealth is evident. The biblical story displays truth in the lives of those whose actions are a faithful response to the ever-demanding, ever-forgiving, ever-fresh summons addressed to the people of God. The truthful life for the Christian is the life of Jesus, and faithful discipleship is the appropriate response. There is no such plumb line in the story of well-being, however, for well-being is the purpose of whatever master image is used. Therefore, if one takes up a master image such as possibility thinking or open marriage and it enhances one's own well-being, the therapeutic character ideal has been fulfilled. The modern person who lives by the therapeutic model does not search for truth or order or coherence. For even if human experience is fundamentally random and incoherent, a story can nevertheless be told, a master image can be invented, that will enhance the sense of well-being, and that is enough.[43]

The question of self-deception is posed somewhat differently for the story of well-being than for the biblical story or the story of success. First of all, the therapeutic tradition does, of course, provide a perspective on self-deception for those who seek therapeutic intervention. Self-deception is understood to be the infliction of pain upon oneself in the belief that one is acting to increase well-being. If at last a person comes to see that actions that are intended to lead to well-being are not leading to well-being at all, but instead inculcate pain and suffering, the therapeutic helper tactfully but persistently enables the sufferer to examine the texture of his or her life and discover which perceptions, which interpretations, and which actions need to be re-visioned so that a more enduring sense of well-being may emerge.

But a more enduring sense of well-being is also the purpose of the cover story. Our real story, fashioned by our underlying sense of how the events in our life connect, is often painful. The cover story, as another way of interpreting our action, is less painful, more honorable, and also plausible. It enhances our own sense of well-being. Cover stories are therefore difficult to distinguish in the culture of well-being, for all stories have the same purpose. Thus self-deception is a characteristic mode of life in contemporary culture.

Arthur Miller's play *Death of a Salesman* is one of the most powerful presentations of the theme of self-deception in American culture. The story is told in terms of a fundamental conflict between "survival of the fittest" and "personality" as master images of the self. The salesman, Willie Loman, believes that a good personality enables a man to get ahead in the business world. A man of spirit fashions his own personality. "Be liked and you will never want" is Willie's word to his boys.

On the other hand, the image of the "survival of the fittest" is also appealing to Willie. Willie's brother Ben lived by the survivalist code and made a fortune doing it. But at last Willie returns to his conviction that "personal-

ity always wins the day." He tells the story of Dave Sin-
gleman, and asks if there could be anything

> more satisfying than to be able to go, at the age of eighty-
> four, into twenty or thirty different cities, and pick up a
> phone, and be remembered and loved and helped by so
> many different people? Do you know? when he died—and by
> the way he died the death of a salesman, in his green velvet
> slippers in the smoker of the New York, New Haven and
> Hartford, going into Boston—when he died, hundreds of
> salesmen and buyers were at his funeral.[44]

To Willie, the wonder of this country is that here a man
can end up with diamonds on the basis of being liked.

In the twilight of his life, Willie is no longer able to
distinguish clearly between his hopes and the reality in
which he lives, between his dreams and his dime-a-dozen
days and dime-a-dozen sons. He cannot tell the difference
between being a man of good character and being a "personality." He is unable to affirm the meaning of being a
person who is also a salesman, a carpenter, a gardener, a
husband, and a father. All that counts for Willie is to be
successful by being well-liked.

Willie Loman's difficulty is that the story of well-being
encourages, indeed develops, his self-deception. There is
no understanding of the limits of life or of the reality of gift
and response. The story of well-being throws him back on
his own resources. A man of spirit can fashion the personality that always wins the day. Failure is therefore personal
failure, because it is the failure of spirit. At this point, the
stories of well-being and success share a common vision.
To succeed is to be a worthwhile person. To fail is to be
worthless. In such a light Willie's suicide makes sense. He
believes that he will be gratefully remembered because he
will achieve his life's goal: financial independence for his
sons. In one decisive act, a worthless life will be transformed by an insurance policy into a worthwhile success.

The tragedy of Willie Loman is not that he is self-
deceived. The biblical story makes it clear that human beings regularly avoid spelling out the true character of their

engagements with the world. The people who own the land, King David, the rich young ruler, and the Christians in Corinth all live in cover stories. To live is to be self-deceived. The tragedy of Willie Loman is that the dominant story of his life provides little training in the skills necessary for recognizing cover stories and saying explicitly what he is doing in the world.

Conclusion

Well-being is now the dominant cultural ethic. In his sharp critique, Lasch argues that narcissistic personality has taken center stage and plays a conspicuous part in contemporary life. The celebrity, basking in the adulation of the masses, sets the tone for public life, not only in the ever-increasing scope of the entertainment industry but also in politics, religion, and business. The primary asset of Ronald Reagan, Robert Schuller, or Lee Iacocca is personality. The boundary between public and private realms disappears, for the celebrity elicits and reinforces the same yearning for well-being in everyone, the fantasy life that consists of "nothing more substantial than a wish to be vastly admired, not for one's accomplishments but simply for oneself, uncritically and without reservation."[45]

Bellah is less pessimistic. He recognizes that the self, set adrift from family, religion, and calling as sources of authority, obligation, and moral example, pursues well-being. In such a world the language of "values" becomes the dead end of radical individualism. But he believes that the people to whom he talks are better than that. Somehow, in spite of the limits of the language of well-being, we know we discover who we are "face to face and side by side with others in work, love and learning." Even our radical individualism is dependent on a cultural context. It is also shaped with and by others. There is still a structure of grace in history.[46]

Resources to live a more truthful life are yet available in American culture. Franklin's story of self-discipline and self-denial for the sake of real accomplishments, both personal and communal, can still be heard. The biblical story of gifts and faithful response to those gifts still echoes in various corners of the land. But it is also true that the dominant ethos, the therapeutic ethos, rejects such visions as illusions or translates them to its own purpose: the vision of an intensely private sense of well-being to be generated in the living of life itself.

5

The Mission of America

"We observe today not a victory of party but a celebration of freedom,"John F. Kennedy declared in the opening lines of his inaugural address. He pointed out that he had sworn the same oath before the people and God that was prescribed in 1787. Although the world was very different in 1961, Kennedy believed that the same revolutionary beliefs for which our forebears fought were still at issue around the globe—"the belief that the rights of man come not from the generosity of the state but from the hand of God." Kennedy then restated, in modern terms, his understanding of the mission of America:

> We dare not forget today that we are the heirs of that first revolution. Let the word go forth from this time and place, to friend and foe alike, that the torch has been passed to a new generation of Americans—born in this century, tempered by war, disciplined by a hard and bitter peace, proud of our ancient heritage—and unwilling to witness or permit the slow undoing of those human rights to which this nation has always been committed, and to which we are committed today at home and around the world.
>
> Let every nation know, whether it wishes us well or ill, that we shall pay any price, bear any burden, meet any hardship, support any friend, oppose any foe to assure the survival and the success of liberty.[1]

Each generation of Americans has been summoned to respond to such a mission, Kennedy reminded his listeners. Now the trumpet has sounded again, summoning us to the struggle against tyranny, poverty, disease, and war. Kennedy concluded, "Since a good conscience is our only sure reward, we will ask God's blessing and help, but knowing that here on earth God's work must truly be our own."[2]

Kennedy's inaugural address sounded a chord that has resonated throughout American history. From the beginning of the settlement of America, Americans have believed they have a special destiny, a worldwide mission. The "mission of America," a historically created system of meaning, has been an unusually powerful pattern in terms of which we Americans have understood our role in the world community, and by which we have shaped and ordered our relationship to other nations. Because the mission-of-America narrative has envisioned a special destiny for the nation but not for the individual or the communities within the nation, it has been a narrative that shapes the understanding of self only insofar as a person acts as a member of the national community. Therefore, the story of the mission of America has fashioned the world of citizen and nation and has given a sense of vocation and purpose to the corporate reality to which Americans have been bound by the "mystic chords of memory."[3]

Since the mission-of-America story includes the American experience from the founding of the colonies to the present, it readily uses images from both the biblical story and the Enlightenment story of progress. In order to fully understand this cultural narrative, we need to examine its basic themes, discuss the conflict that arises between them, and then reflect on how the evangelical theme of the mission of America became the cultural narrative in terms of which presidents such as Kennedy summoned the nation to war.

America as Example and as Leader

Russel B. Nye suggests that the story of the mission of America has been told in a remarkably constant way throughout most of American history. There are two basic themes in this story: (1) the exemplary theme—the United

States serves as an example to the rest of the nations of God's plan for the world, and as proof that a people can govern themselves in peace and justice; and (2) the evangelical theme—the United States assumes the responsibility to defend or extend the freedom of all peoples, leading others toward a future world state of freedom and liberty as yet unknown.[4]

The mission story gave early Americans a sense of corporate meaning and purpose. To leave Europe was to leave civilization, family, a sense of history, and an order of life. To arrive in America was to arrive in a land in which only a few small towns separated vast tracts of wilderness. The mission story provided individuals with a sense of history in a new corporate body. Whether they lived in the biblical story or the story of success, individuals were bound together as Americans, as a people who shared a special destiny. The conviction that their new nation had a unique mission to the world gave the ordinary citizen a way of investing the ordinary round of democratic duties with world significance.[5]

America as Example

The mission of America has been expressed in the language and metaphors of both the biblical story and the Enlightenment story of progress. When Americans first began to think with the biblical story, they saw themselves as chosen people, who, like Israel of old, had experienced an exodus and had been given a new land. They were to live in the new land in the liberty that God intended, free from the bondage and corruption of the past. As American history began to unfold, however, the events of that history seemed to be more than a rehearsal of the past. The old images of exodus and promised land were no longer adequate. The Puritans began to interpret the American experience with images of the future: that is, with millennial images.

Christians traditionally understood the millennium to be the thousand years at the end of history during which

Christ would reign over the world. The millennium would therefore be a thousand-year period of justice and peace. But in America, Puritans came to believe that God intended for Christians themselves to establish a just and peaceful society. After the just society endured for a thousand years, Christ would come to bring history to a close. This millennial interpretation of history at first found its strongest advocates in New England. After the Great Awakenings, millennialism became widespread in the colonies.[6]

Millennial thought became one of the primary ways of expressing the exemplary theme of the mission of America. The direction of world history was thought to depend upon the response of Americans to the signs of providence that the millennium was at hand. Two events seemed to Puritans to be signs that the thousand years of peace and justice were at hand: (1) the first Great Awakening, with revivals that were renewing the church and binding Americans together as one people, and (2) the Revolution, which provided a government that would no longer oppress the people, but rule justly. The future was now marked by hope. Americans began to expect the coming perfection of history, and its nearness could be seen in the signs of the present. America, with its great revivals and revolution, was surely the example of God's plan for mankind.[7]

The majority of the clergy took up this new millennial point of view. Jonathan Edwards, one of the leading Puritans, spoke for many Christians in his sermon, "The Latter-Day Glory Is Probably to Begin in America." Edwards pointed out that scripture promises that God will create a new heaven and a new earth. The discovery of America, the Great Awakening, and the revolution were signs that God had begun to create a new world in a spiritual respect. Those whose eyes were open could see clearly that the revolution was not simply a political event. The revolution was the greatest unveiling of God's purposes since the Reformation. Divine providence was calling America to be an example to the world, to be the first new nation of the new age. Thus by using the doctrine of the calling, Edwards easily moved from the biblical story's image of the faithful self to the mission-of-America's image of the faithful nation. If America was faithful to her calling and became a nation that displayed true religion, wisdom, and liberty, then surely all could hope that the millennium was at hand.[8]

The mission of America was expressed in millennial images until the Civil War. American churches continued to teach that America was God's new Israel, created by God as a sign of the millennium. Thus for the American church the nation itself was invested with extraordinary religious significance. This belief reflected on the churches. American Christians, divided into denominations and sects with many different ways of interpreting the biblical story, were nonetheless united through their special nation with its special calling from God.[9]

The millennial vision of the American churches engendered a passion for public reform throughout the first half of the nineteenth century. The second Great Awakening confirmed in many Americans the belief that they were called by God to perfect the world. But before they went out to the world, Americans were convinced that they must first create a godly society at home. This commitment inspired the organizing of religious and moral associations to preach the gospel, establish schools and Sunday schools, and achieve larger social goals: end the oppression of blacks, women, and workers; improve the factory system, prison conditions, and education; and work for temperance and world peace. Thus the churches provided both the demand that each citizen should seek the good of the whole community and the institutional means of exercising such a citizenship. Through such a process, the churches connected the doctrine of the individual's calling to serve the community to the calling of the nation to be an example to the world.[10]

The conviction that America was an example to the world was also proclaimed in the idiom of the Enlightenment. Americans imagined that both the individual and the nation could progress through the discovery of and faithful adherence to the laws that govern the universe. As we have seen in the story of success, this faith in progress was readily taken up as an individual image of self and world. But it was also applied to the nation.

As previously noted, the clearest application of the Enlightenment faith to the new nation appeared in the Declaration of Independence. The equality of all persons and the right to life, liberty, and the pursuit of happiness were considered to be self-evident to persons of reason. Further, the Declaration placed the revolution in the broad sweep of universal history, with import far beyond the relationship between Britain and her colonies. It was not British law to which the Declaration appealed, but "the laws of Nature and of Nature's God." Jefferson's concern to pay a "decent respect to the opinions of mankind" underlined the conviction of the Enlightenment thinkers that America was to be an example to all the nations.[11]

The faith of Jefferson and his colleagues in the orderliness of the universe also led them to reflect that order in the institutions of government that followed the Declaration. The notion that such a body as a constitutional convention could create a constitutional government by the exercise of reason rested, in large part, upon faith in the Enlightenment story of progress. Since Jefferson believed that all persons of reason shared that faith, he argued to his dying day that American institutions made America an example to the whole world, for they restored "the free right to the unbounded exercise of reason and freedom of opinion. All eyes are opened, or opening, to the rights of man. . . . These are the grounds of hope for others."[12]

America as Leader

The second theme of the mission of America was evangelical. In this vision, America had a responsibility to enable all nations to gain freedom. The patriots of '76 believed their revolution had a universal quality. They thought America was an example for all mankind to follow. They were not obsessed with the unique character of America. They invited all idealists and refugees from the

Old World to join them, and all nations to share their vision.[13]

But by mid-century Americans had narrowed their vision. They were convinced that America had its own unique manifest destiny. According to William McLoughlin, Americans slowly developed the conviction that they were a new and special race, and that the democracy they had fashioned was beyond the abilities of "decadent Europeans, superstitious Roman Catholics, ignorant heathen, or 'colored races' to imitate." Americans believed that God had created America and called her to establish democracy throughout the world. They were to teach inferior peoples the ways of Christian America.[14]

The conviction that America had a manifest destiny to extend and export the American way was often expressed in either the language of biblical story or the images of the story of progress. Speaking out of the story of progress, Emerson wrote that "the office of America is to liberate, to abolish kingcraft, priestcraft, caste, monopoly, to pull down the gallows . . . wherever these may be." As did many others, Herman Melville intertwined the themes of race and country in his understanding of the mission of America. In *White Jacket,* Melville seemed sure that Americans were the new Israel, God's peculiar, chosen people. This, however, was only a beginning:

> God has predestined, mankind expects, great things from our race; and great things we feel in our souls. The rest of the nations must soon be in our rear. . . . Long enough have we been sceptics with regard to ourselves, and doubted whether, indeed, the political Messiah had come. But he has come in *us,* if we would but give utterance to his promptings. And let us always remember that with ourselves, almost for the first time in the history of earth, national selfishness is unbounded philanthropy; for we cannot do a good to America, but we give alms to the world.[15]

The sentiments of Emerson and Melville were widespread. Americans such as Daniel Webster, Henry Clay, James Monroe, and John Calhoun responded to the uprisings in Europe in the early nineteenth century with speeches of encouragement. Mass meetings were held to raise arms for the revolutionaries. It seemed evident to most Americans that America was to improve the state of the world.

The Conflict Between the Themes

Whether the world was to be improved by means of American arms was not so clear. It was not clear because of the conflict between the two facets of the mission. Those like Washington and Jefferson, who argued for the exemplary mission, were convinced that America was an example to all nations because America had left behind the tragedy of endless war.

Washington and Jefferson both believed that a wise providence had set a great gulf between America and the armed conflicts of Europe. In his farewell address, Washington argued that our "detached and distant situation" enabled us to pursue a different course from Europe's "ambition, rivalship, interest, humor or caprice." Jefferson was convinced that, as part of the American "experiment," Americans had turned their backs on Europe, which was composed of "nations of eternal war." Jefferson believed that the American people, with so favorable a chance of trying "the opposite system, of peace and fraternity with mankind," would surely choose the path of reason.[16]

On the other hand, those who saw America from the perspective of the evangelical mission were convinced that the nation needed to go to the aid of oppressed peoples. If America was to be committed to human rights around the world, then America must pay the price, bear the burden, and meet the hardship of the struggle against tyranny even if that meant war.

John Quincy Adams understood this threat of war as a conflict between the exemplary and evangelical facets of the mission of America. He sought to resolve the conflict in favor of the exemplary mission. In an address in 1821, Adams argued that America ought to support the standard of freedom and independence wherever it might be unfurled. That support, however, must be characterized by the presence of America's heart, prayers, voice, and example. America must not send armed forces. America must not go abroad in search of monsters to destroy, for if Americans enlisted under banners other than their own, America would become involved beyond the power of extrication in the endless wars of interest, intrigue, ambition, and empire that "assume the colors and usurp the standards of freedom."[17]

Kennedy's inaugural address makes it clear that the arguments of Washington, Jefferson, and Adams have not put to rest the conflict between the exemplary and the evangelical themes in the mission of America. The statements of presidents in time of war and the Cold War read like a serialized story of the mission of America from the evangelical perspective. Abraham Lincoln is the only president who goes beyond the images and metaphors of the mission of America as he thinks about the involvement of America in war.

The most common images used to justify the Civil War were metaphors of holy war. The Civil War was fought as a crusade by both North and South. Lincoln, however, argued that God was not a crusader. The Almighty designed history in light of an eternal perspective, to which the angry passions of warring peoples were blind. God's ordering of human life was one that took up both judgment and grace for North and South alike. Therefore, in his second inaugural, Lincoln spoke against the single vision of the crusaders:

> The Almighty has His own purposes. "Woe unto the world because of offenses! for it must needs be that offenses come; but woe to that man by whom the offense cometh."
>
> ... Fondly do we hope, fervently do we pray, that this mighty scourge of war may speedily pass away.
>
> Yet, if God wills that it continue until all the wealth piled by the bondsman's 250 years of unrequited toil shall be sunk, and until every drop of blood drawn with the lash shall be paid by another drawn with the sword, as was said 3,000

years ago, so still it must be said, "the judgments of the Lord are true and righteous altogether."[18]

No other president viewed America's involvement in war from such a perspective, however. James Madison, James Polk, William McKinley, Woodrow Wilson, Franklin D. Roosevelt, Harry Truman, Kennedy, Lyndon Johnson, Richard Nixon, and Reagan all have argued for the evangelical mission of America.

The Evangelical Theme and America's Wars

As we attempt to understand the character of moral debate in America, we need, then, to spend a considerable time seeking to understand how the evangelical mission shapes the American corporate understanding of self and world. Like the exemplary theme, the evangelical mission is a community story. In this sense, both the exemplary and evangelical themes stand against the individualistic images of self and world that arise out of the stories of success or well-being. But Americans respond to the two themes in very different ways.

On the one hand, as Americans dwell in the metaphors of the exemplary theme, they envision the good community. It seems self-evident to Americans that they, as members of the national community, should go about the task of bringing the reality of America in line with its hopes and its ideals. Although biblical images are dominant, Americans take up both biblical and Enlightenment images in their understanding of that task. The common language of the exemplary theme provides an understanding of self and world that is rooted in a constructive vision of community.

On the other hand, as Americans live in the story of the evangelical theme, their life as a community is characterized by aggressive actions toward other peoples. But since aggression is not consonant with the way Americans want to see themselves, a cover story is required. The claim is made that if Americans annex a territory or take over a government, they are giving the people of those lands the institutions of liberty. For this reason Reinhold Niebuhr argues that the most significant moral characteristic of the nation is self-deception. In telling the story of the evangelical theme of the mission of America, the nation draws about itself the cloak of the sacred, claims that its values are the highest civilized values, and, as it goes to war, affirms that the whole enterprise of humanity is involved in its struggle.[19]

To deepen our understanding of how war has come to be seen as a virtue in American culture, we need to reflect briefly on the wars of America. In light of the human tendency toward self-deception, it is no surprise to discover that Americans, who thought they had left war behind, are as warlike as other nations. What is surprising is the way Americans justify their involvement in war. Because the founders of the nation believed that America, the example to all nations, was leaving the insane evil of war behind, one might expect that when America went to war it would be seen as a tragic departure from America's hopes and ideals.

However, only a minority of Americans understand war as tragedy. Instead, tragic action is usually characterized as action in which persons or communities have consciously chosen evil for the sake of the good, and have taken upon themselves the burden of guilt for the doing of evil that good may come. The evil that is done is faced and accepted, and in the case of war, the consequences of evil done by war are weighed against the consequences of allowing a situation of oppression to continue.

From within the biblical story, the "just war" advocates have usually taken account of the tragic nature of the human condition by such a weighing of the consequences. They understand themselves to be in a situation in which all choices entail the doing of evil, and therefore even the doing of what good can be done entails guilt. Although those taking up the just war position do not believe they can avoid guilt, they do believe they can reduce suffering if war is carefully restricted.

The just war position has been recently restated by the American Catholic bishops in a pastoral letter. The bishops point out that the moral theory if the just war begins with the presumption that binds all Christians: We should do no harm to our neighbor; how we treat our enemy is the key test of how we love our neighbor; and the taking of even one human life is a prospect that we should consider in fear and trembling. Yet a Christian is also morally bound to defend the innocent. The moral questions are, "How shall the innocent be defended and peace be restored?"[20]

The bishops recognize that nonviolent resistance to evil is perhaps the primary way for Christians to defend the innocent and restore peace. The argument of Martin Luther King, Jr., and Dorothy Day, that biblical story demands nonviolent resistance to evil, is persuasive. King and Day point out that nonviolent resisters seek to right the wrong and heal the community through the same action. Love stands at the center of nonviolent resistance. Nonviolent resisters refuse to cooperate with oppressive regimes. Not only physical violence but violence of the spirit is avoided. Since Jesus both taught and lived such a love, believers in nonviolent resistance to evil have a great hope in the truth of their witness.[21]

Because nonviolent resisters follow Jesus with such faith and such hope, the bishops rightly note that nonviolent resistance to evil is a fundamental Christian response. But because nonviolence requires such a personal commitment, it is an appropriate response only for individuals and churches. Drawing upon natural law theory, the bishops argue that the state must use arms to protect the innocent.

The bishops believe it is moral for a state to take up arms to defend the innocent and restore peace only if the war is a just war. A just war is a war with limited purposes. The war must oppose real and certain danger, protect innocent life, and reduce suffering. If suffering is to be reduced, nations must take serious account of three aspects of war: (1) The goal of the war must be to establish the conditions necessary for decent human existence and basic human rights. Wars that are fought to defend oppressive regimes can never be considered just. (2) The damage to be inflicted and the costs incurred by the war must be proportionate to the good expected upon taking up arms. Unnecessarily destructive acts or unreasonable conditions such as unconditional surrender must be avoided. (3) Nations at war must discriminate between combatants and noncombatants. Intentional attacks on noncombatants and nonmilitary targets are prohibited. Therefore, entire classes of human beings, such as all persons in a city, can never be justly attacked. Although these criteria seek to reduce the terror of war and limit suffering, war still requires the killing of other persons. Therefore, war, even just war, always involves the doing of evil for the sake of the good, and thus is tragic.[22]

The motivations and intentions that underlie America's wars are not usually expressed in the language of tragedy or of just war, but in the language of the crusade. The crusade is justified in terms of religious and ideological motivations rather than political and practical ones. It is fought on behalf of an ideal. Such motivations define the cause as holy, the crusaders as righteous, and the enemy as the incarnation of evil. The holy cause for the wars of America has been the evangelical mission of America. Underneath the crusade language, however, a real story that is neither righteous nor honorable has been acted out.[23]

The evangelical mission of America is the cover story for the wars of America. The wars that reveal the sharpest discontinuity between the cover story and the real story in the nineteenth century are the war against Mexico in 1846 and the war against Spain in 1898. The war in Vietnam reveals the largest difference between the cover story and the real story in the twentieth century. Although none of the wars in which America has been involved will pass examination as a just war, it is worthwhile to reflect upon the wars in which the nation has been most clearly involved in self-deception. One hopes such an examination will enable us to see how the cover story is used in the public justification of each war.

The War Against Mexico

Most Americans saw the war with Mexico as part of America's "manifest destiny." Manifest destiny was a term that captured in a single, arresting slogan much of the feelings generated by the evangelical mission of America. Manifest destiny was the application of the evangelical mission to the North American continent. In 1845, John L. Sullivan, editor of the *Democratic Review,* argued that the true title to Oregon and Texas belonged to America "by the right of our manifest destiny to overspread and to possess the whole of the continent which Providence has given us for the development of the great experiment of liberty and federative self government entrusted to us." Manifest destiny included the themes of providence, progress, and expansion. For some, "expansion" meant expansion westward; for others it was expansion across the whole continent; and for others, the whole hemisphere.[24]

For many of those living in the biblical story, if expansion was ordained of God, it ought to be awaited with patience. It would take a generation or more for Americans to move into a territory, improve the land, teach the people there the value of freedom, and train them in the practice of the democratic way. For, according to the peaceful vision of the mission of America, only when neighboring peoples were ready would they apply for admission to the "temple of freedom."

President Polk, who took office in 1845, put forth a much more activistic interpretation of manifest destiny. He intended that California should enter the Union. When Mexico refused Polk's attempt to negotiate the recognition of the Rio Grande del Norte as the southern boundary of the United States, Polk ordered American forces to occupy the left bank of the Rio Grande. Mexico demanded that they withdraw, and when they refused, Mexican cavalry attacked a troop of United States dragoons. Upon receiving reports of the skirmish, Polk sent a war message to Congress.

Polk's message stirred considerable dissent in Congress.

Calhoun asked whether a local skirmish constituted war between two nations. John Quincy Adams led the opposition in the House. Later, Congressman Abraham Lincoln contended that Polk had deceived the American people. But the majority of Americans believed in manifest destiny. The antiwar forces in Congress were readily defeated, for to oppose so popular a public sentiment was to court electoral defeat.

Both Mexicans and Americans knew the American demand was but an opening salvo in a conflict that would determine whether much of northwest Mexico would become southwest United States. California, the beautiful and fertile land on the Pacific shore, had been receiving increased American immigration during the 1840s. For at least a generation before the Mexican-American War, Americans had expressed their desire for California. The desire arose out of the recognition that California's ports provided access to vast maritime opportunities, the continuing demand for more land to settle, and a yearning to see America fill the continent.

The eagerness for California increased as the expansionist press anticipated war. In July, 1845, the *Hartford Times* had declared that if America should be called to a conquest of Mexico by commencement of hostilities on Mexico's part,

> we shall believe the call is from heaven; that we are called to redeem from unhallowed hands a *land,* above all others, favored of heaven, and to hold it for the use of a people who know how to obey heaven's behests.[25]

The racist aspect of such declarations of manifest destiny was not lost on Mexicans. They well knew that Americans looked upon Mexicans as an inferior people, and that they had no regard for the human rights nor the culture of those they considered inferior. Mexico was determined to oppose manifest destiny, even though Mexico was no military match for the United States. Just before the outbreak of hostilities, President Herrera stated that Mexico was in no "condition to wage war and in no mood to preserve the peace at the price of concessions." But he could avoid nei-

ther war nor defeat nor the concession of more than a
third of Mexico. By September of 1847, American troops
entered Mexico City. In February of 1848, the Treaty of
Guadalupe Hidalgo secured California for the United
States.[26]

Manifest Destiny: A Cover Story

Manifest destiny is a cover story that assumes the form
of the biblical story but empties it of the substance. The
form is that of a covenant story: Providence has blessed
and will continue to bless Americans with a good land. But
there is within manifest destiny no story that displays the
character of the divine provider, or demands that the character of the chosen people be conformed to the provider.
There is no concern for the "stranger," no passion for justice, and no year of jubilee in which debts will be canceled
and slaves set free. Manifest destiny is a story of a gift-
giving providence that does not ask or require the recipients to be gift-givers as well.

Manifest destiny was the cover story for the Mexican-
American War. The real story was the story of expansion.
From its founding, America had experienced a steady flow
of population westward. The vanguard of that movement
was already establishing settlements in the Willamette Valley of Oregon and the central valley of California. The
story of the evangelical mission of America used the language of manifest destiny to justify the displacement or
destruction of both Mexicans and native Americans.

Josiah Royce, who wrote one of the earliest histories of
California, suggested that

> the American as conqueror is unwilling to appear in public
> as a pure aggressor; he dare not seize a California as Russia
> had seized so much land in Asia. The American wants to
> persuade not only the world, but himself, that he is doing
> God service in a peaceable Spirit, even when he violently
> takes what he has determined to get. His conscience is sensi-
> tive, and hostile aggression, practiced against any but Indi-
> ans, shocks this conscience, unused as it is to such scenes.[27]

Royce apparently believed that the confession of sin was the beginning of wisdom, even for historians.[28]

Self-deception is the "persuasion of the self" of which Royce speaks. Aggression and conquest are actions that are not compatible with Americans' view of themselves. The use of manifest destiny provides another way of interpreting America's action, a less painful, more honorable, and also plausible way. An examination of the war from the perspective of justice is, however, much less gratifying. Certainly there was no real and certain danger to be opposed, and the reduction of suffering was not the aim pursued; all peaceful means of conflict resolution were not exhausted. Like the stories of success and well-being, the evangelical theme of the mission of America projects an image of self and world that has little ability to deal with self-deception. Royce's conclusion is assuredly the thoughtful one: confession of sin is the beginning of wisdom.

The Spanish-American War

The story of the evangelical mission of America also served as the cover story for the Spanish-American War in 1898. In his discussion of the war, Augustus Cerillo, Jr., examines the economic context and the impact of Social Darwinism and racism on the attitudes of Americans toward the war. In the latter part of the nineteenth century, industrialization, urbanization, and immigration were placing severe strains upon American society. The frontier closed; a harsh depression added millions to the ranks of the jobless; there was much labor unrest, such as the strike at Homestead; demands for relief increased from farmers and labor; and the populist and socialist movements were attracting more and more persons to their programs of social reform. One attractive answer to the difficulties of the times lay in the development of new world markets. The capital-rich entrepreneurs such as Carnegie were eager to invest overseas.[29]

President McKinley learned the art of politics in this era of expansionism. In his first inaugural address, President

McKinley stated, "We want no wars of conquest; we must avoid the temptations of territorial aggression." Yet, by the close of the Spanish-American War, what had begun as a crusade to liberate Cuba from the tyranny of Spain had become an American war of conquest. America had acquired Puerto Rico, Guam, the Philippines, and the right of intervention "for the protection of life, property, and individual liberty" in Cuba.

During this period Americans began to fashion a global manifest destiny. To the traditional theme of the evangelical mission was added a blend of Social Darwinism, economic expansionism, and Anglo-Saxon racism. One of the most articulate spokesmen for this point of view was Senator Albert J. Beveridge of Indiana.

Beveridge argued that Americans were God's chosen people, who could not be dishonest in seeking empire but who dared not shirk "the purpose of a fate that has driven us to be greater than our small institutions." Therefore, Americans must not retreat from "any soil where Providence has unfurled her banner. . . . In the tide of God's great purposes, the present phase may be to our personal profit," but the "far-off end is the redemption of the world and the Christianization of mankind." The need for government as a partner in overseas expansion seemed critical. Russia, Germany, France, and Great Britain were all dividing the Asian markets into spheres of influence. If America was to continue to be the voice of liberty for the whole world, "the sovereign factor in the peace of the world," said Beveridge, the American republic must exercise commercial supremacy. Beveridge was convinced, and many others agreed with him, that politics, commerce, and providence all required the same mission of America."[30]

Josiah Strong was one of the best known of the clergy who suggested that manifest destiny was a global doctrine. In his book *Our Country,* Strong argued that every race that strongly impressed itself upon world history has possessed a great idea. The Anglo-Saxon race gained an edge in the competitive struggle because it developed two great ideas: liberty and a pure, spiritual Christianity. Strong agreed with Herbert Spencer: "From biological truths it is to be inferred that . . . the Americans may reasonably look forward to a time when they have produced a civilization grander than any the world has known." Because of these ideas, this edge, Strong was sure that the Anglo-Saxon race sustained a "peculiar relation to the world's future," for it was "divinely commissioned to be, in a peculiar sense, his brother's keeper." God was training the Anglo-Saxon race in America for a mission to the whole world, and preparing the world to receive that mission.[31]

Strong's fusion of religion, racism, and nationalism was common among religious leaders, so President McKinley knew he was on home ground as he explained to a group of Methodist ministers how he decided to keep the Philippines following the war. He told the ministers that he often prayed to God for guidance concerning the Philippines:

> And one night late it came to me this way—I don't know how it was, but it came: (1) That we could not give them back to Spain—that would be cowardly and dishonorable; (2) that we could not turn them over to France or Germany—our commercial rivals in the Orient—that would be bad business and discreditable; (3) that we could not leave them to themselves—they were unfit for self-government— and they would soon have anarchy and misrule over there worse than Spain's was; and (4) that there was nothing left for us to do but to take them all, and to educate the Filipinos, and uplift and civilize and Christianize them, and by God's grace do the very best we could by them, as our fellowmen for whom Christ also died. And then I went to bed, and went to sleep, and slept soundly.[32]

McKinley did not mention to the ministers that the United States had gone to war against a fairly well organized indigenous independence movement to secure control of the islands. The war lasted three and one half years.

Like the war with Mexico, the Spanish-American War was a war whose cover story was manifest destiny and whose real story was expansionism. The contrast between the cover story and the real story was so sharp that Reinhold Niebuhr was led to remark that the "Spanish Ameri-

can War offers some of the most striking illustrations of
the hypocrisy of governments." Once again it was clear
that the evangelical theme of the mission of America, like
the story of success and well-being, was a story with little
power to work against self-deception.[33]

The Change in Crusade Language

Crusade language underwent a major change in the
twentieth century. In the opening years of World War I,
Wilson was convinced that the role of America was to me-
diate the conflict and reestablish peace. "America is the
only nation which can sympathetically lead the world in
organizing peace," Wilson stated early in the war. "It is
surely the manifest destiny of the United States to lead in
this attempt to make this spirit prevail."[34]

Once America entered the war, however, Wilson himself
had an unusual ability to imagine the war in terms congenial to the mission of America. He argued that the war was
(1) a war to make the world safe for democracy, (2) a war
to end war, (3) a war to protect liberalism, (4) a war against
militarism, (5) a war to redeem barbarous Europe from the
curse of militarism and war, and that (6) therefore, the war
was a crusade. The crusade language at last overcame most
of the opposition to the war, with the notable exception of
the socialists, and Americans went to war to end war and
to make the world safe for democracy.[35]

There was a reaction to the crusade language following
World War I. For the first time America's faith in her mission to the world suffered severe erosion. The disclosure of
the enormous profits made by some Eastern banking and
industrial interests during the war, the failure of the
League of Nations, the worldwide depression, the quick
return of militarism, and the arms race on the international scene made it seem as though all the sacrifices of the
war were in vain. Driven in part by the loss of a corporate
sense of purpose, Americans of the 1920s turned to the
radical individualism of the story of well-being.[36]

Partially because of the public reaction in the aftermath

of World War I, Roosevelt responded to the outbreak of World War II with actions that only slowly and publicly involved the United States in the conflict. After Pearl Harbor, however, Roosevelt was able to articulate the purposes of the war in terms of the mission of America:

> The militarists in Berlin and Tokyo started this war. But the massed, angered forces of common humanity will finish it. . . . Our own objectives are clear: . . . the objective of liberating the subjugated nations—the objective of establishing and securing freedom of speech, freedom of religion, freedom from want, and freedom from fear everywhere in the world.[37]

Wilson and Franklin Roosevelt entered war slowly and publicly. Eisenhower, Kennedy, and Johnson entered the war in Vietnam slowly and covertly. Even in the midst of a massive military buildup in Vietnam, Johnson continued to deceive the Congress and the public as to the extent of the American commitment. Nixon, in turn, secretly widened the war. Although the differences in approach to war had much to do with the difference in the character of the presidents, it also had much to do with the different understandings of the evangelical mission of America.

For the first half of the century, the mission of America was to spread democracy, and therefore, war was justified in such language. In the latter half of the century, however, the emphasis shifted from spreading democracy to opposing communism. As Kennedy put it, America was required to oppose the ambitions of Russia and China for world domination. Kennedy saw that "a cold and secret war" posed a grave dilemma for a free and open society, but he was convinced that America must engage in secret war or "be swept away with the debris of history." Kennedy declared that no greater task faced America or his administration than the struggle against the "rising din of Communist voices." To oppose a secretive, powerful, and ambitious foe, American presidents executed their understanding of the mission of America in a secretive, powerful, and ambitious style.[38]

The primary mark of the new style of the evangelical

mission is the armed struggle for control of a country. According to American policymakers, however, control is not the final purpose. Once America is firmly in control of an area, then efforts will be made to increase the well-being and liberty of the people there. But in war, control becomes the first priority, for without control America cannot refashion a nation.

In the stalemate of the Cold War, however, control is never secure. Therefore, alliances are made with repressive dictatorial regimes to oppose communism. The increase of liberty is postponed. America continues to send troops abroad and to participate in the cycle of endless war. It is a story that the founders did not anticipate. Yet it is a story whose roots were nourished from the beginning by the evangelical theme of the story of the mission of America.

The War in Vietnam and Its Cover Story

It was this Cold War version of the mission of America that carried America into the war in Vietnam. This version of the mission story, borrowing images from the story of well-being, stressed the self-interest of America. Therefore, the Cold War mission was, first of all, to oppose communism; second, to support any "friend," whether democrat or dictator, who would join in opposition to communism; third, if possible, when communism was defeated, extend democracy. President Kennedy summed up the American policy when he outlined the action the United States would take in the Dominican Republic after the assassination of the dictator Trujillo Molina:

> There are three possibilities in descending order of preference: a decent democratic regime, a continuation of the Trujillo regime or a Castro regime. We ought to aim at the first, but we really can't renounce the second until we are sure that we can avoid the third.[39]

This narrowed, second-best mission of America provided the impetus for the American involvement in Vietnam. Following their defeat at Dien Bien Phu in 1954, the

French determined to withdraw from Vietnam after the nationwide elections in 1956. But the Eisenhower administration, convinced that Ho Chi Minh would win the elections, refused the French plan and announced it would "take all steps necessary . . . to defeat communism, to demonstrate that ultimate victory will be won by the free world."[40]

The first necessary step was the creation of South Vietnam as an independent country with a head of state dependent upon the United States. The *Pentagon Papers* historian writes:

> South Vietnam . . . was essentially the creation of the United States.
> Without U.S. support Diem almost certainly could not have consolidated his hold on the South. . . .
> Without the threat of U.S. intervention, South Vietnam could not have refused to even discuss the elections called for in 1956 . . . without being immediately overrun by the Viet Minh armies.
> Without U.S. aid in the years following, the Diem regime certainly, and an independent South Vietnam almost as certainly, could not have survived.[41]

Kennedy continued the same policy, but he was troubled by the Buddhist protests against the repressive policies of Diem. Nonetheless, the policy was reaffirmed and the argument made that, if South Vietnam went communist, the rest of Southeast Asia would go communist as well. As a result, 15,000 United States troops were sent to South Vietnam.[42]

In *Vantage Point,* Lyndon Johnson argued that his policy in Vietnam was the same as Kennedy's. But Johnson was not troubled by the repressive tactics of the South Vietnamese government. Johnson believed that the real issue was aggression by the North Vietnamese, and that the world had learned at Munich that aggression must be firmly resisted. Johnson was certain aggression could be discouraged by raising the "costs."[43]

Johnson failed to consider that Munich and World War

II involved the defense of the Western democracies and
Vietnam involved the defense of a repressive dictatorial
regime. He continued to proclaim that the war in Vietnam
was a war for freedom and democracy, a war like the
American Revolutionary War. Johnson's failure to see the
difference between America's involvement in the two wars
demonstrates the change in the character of the mission of
America. The primary purpose of America was no longer
to encourage the spread of freedom and democracy but to
oppose communism.[44]

The vast majority of Americans agreed with Johnson.
The change in the mission of America seemed to the majority a natural and necessary response to communism. As
late as 1968, only 35 percent of Americans believed the
American involvement in the war was wrong. Not until
1970, when it was clear that America could not win, did 56
percent of the American people express the feeling that the
war was a mistake.[45]

The costs of the war, however, began to change the perspective of some of the policymakers. Secretary of Defense
Robert McNamara, appalled by the increasing rate of civil-
ian casualties, ordered a review of America's involvement
in Vietnam. Senator William Fulbright, chairman of the
Senate Foreign Relations Committee, argued that America
was not at war to establish democracy and freedom, but
for two basic reasons: "the view of communism as an evil
philosophy and the view of ourselves as God's avenging
angels, whose sacred duty it is to combat evil philosophies." Fulbright pointed out that historically power con-
fuses itself with virtue. A powerful nation often comes to
believe it has a special destiny to fashion the world in its
own image. Fulbright suggested that this point of view corresponds to the evangelical mission of America and urged
the nation to return to the exemplary view.[46]

Senators Eugene McCarthy and Robert Kennedy opposed the war by challenging President Johnson in the
Democratic presidential primaries. In his last speech in the
United States Senate, Robert Kennedy challenged the
moral right of America to continue the war. He questioned

whether we have the authority to kill tens of thousands of persons because we say we have a commitment to the South Vietnamese people. He inquired, "But have they been consulted—in Hue, in Ben Tre, in other towns that have been destroyed? . . . What we have been doing is not the answer, it is not suitable, and it is immoral, and intolerable to continue it."[47]

Richard Nixon promised "peace with honor" but widened the war by offensives into Cambodia and Laos, and intensified bombing. An armistice was negotiated in January of 1973. In effect, the agreement permitted the North to take over the South through either elections or military action. Speaking in direct opposition to the earlier American views, Secretary of State Henry Kissinger remarked that if one group of Vietnamese proved superior to the other "that is no American concern." In the spring of 1975 the North Vietnamese Army entered Saigon and unified Vietnam under communist control.

The cover story used during the war in Vietnam is the story of the mission of America to be the champion of the "free world" against the ambitions of the communist leaders. America saw itself and all who would support America as truly righteous, and all others as truly evil. The sad succession of repressive regimes in South Vietnam were thereby considered to be part of the "free world." The war destroyed the traditional bases of Vietnamese society, the village and the family. Much of the population was resettled into slums near army installations or cities like Saigon. Nearly all the able-bodied men of South Vietnam were hired with American money to fight a war for a government established by American power. Nevertheless, American presidents proclaimed the war to be one like the American Revolution. The self-deceit that began with Eisenhower and continued with Kennedy became a primary way of governing the nation under Johnson and Nixon. It culminated in Watergate. The evangelical mission of America had become a story of self-deceit, and by living in that story year after year, the American government became an example of deceit rather than of democracy.

The real story of America has been a story of gifts and of limits. America achieved its position as a world power not because of its virtue, but because of its many gifts. The gift of isolation from the warring powers of Europe in the early years of the nation enabled the country to develop its own institutions without being required to invest large resources in a military establishment. Factors as diverse as the Great Awakenings and the gift of wise leadership in its founding years made possible the development of a consensus concerning the form of government. Incredibly rich natural resources enabled the nation to respond quickly to the industrial revolution. World War I transformed the nation from a secondary power to a major power. World War II reduced the rest of the industrial world to shambles but did not reach the American shores. The United States emerged as the preeminent military and industrial power in the world.

The history of the exercise of that power demonstrated that even vast economic and military power has limits. In Vietnam, the United States brought an unimaginable amount of military power to bear on an ancient rural society. Much was destroyed. Little was created. And thereby the limits of power were displayed in two ways. First, as George Kennan has noted, in Vietnam there was a "failure to appreciate the limitations of war in general—any war— as a vehicle for the advancements of the objectives of the democratic state." Although war may at times be necessary, the democratic purpose has not prospered when people have died or an army has been defeated; it prospers only when something happens to increase a person's enlightenment and consciousness of her or his relationship to other people—something that makes the person aware that, whenever the dignity of another person is offended, one's own dignity is thereby reduced.[48]

Second, because of the limits of war in advancing the democratic purpose, the change in the evangelical mission from establishing democracy to opposing communism resulted in a loss of corporate meaning. The mission of America no longer gave ordinary citizens a way of investing the basic duties of democratic citizenship with world significance. Democracy was no longer spread by example. With the decline in meaning of the mission of America, individuals came to rely more and more on the story of well-being for their sense of self and world. The concern of the sixties that America renew freedom at home and abroad faded into the "me first" perspective of the eighties.

Rethinking the Nuclear Arms Race

The nuclear arms race threatens to destroy human life. For many people, that threat adds new urgency to the debate about the mission of America. In recent years, both the bishops of the Roman Catholic Church in America and the bishops of the United Methodist Church have written pastoral letters outlining what they believe to be the Christian response to the threat of the nuclear arms race. An examination of these two letters allows us to see how two churches, rather than particular individuals, bring the resources of biblical story to bear on the question of the nuclear arms race.

In *The Challenge of Peace*, the Catholic bishops begin by thinking with the biblical tradition about war. On one hand, the bishops make it clear that Jesus not only taught peace, but that his resurrection "is the sign to the world that God indeed does reign, does give life in death, and that the love of God is stronger even than death" (Rom. 8:36–39).[49] Only in light of this resurrection power can Jesus' gift of peace be understood. The bishops are convinced, therefore, that "Jesus Christ, then, is our peace. . . . In him God has reconciled the world, made it one . . . his will is this reconciliation, this unity between God and all peoples, and among the peoples themselves."[50]

On the other hand, the bishops argue that God's peace is an eschatological peace, a peace that is not yet fully present. Therefore, in the age in which we do live, although individuals may choose to be pacifists, governments have the responsibility to protect the innocent, even if that means war. But any war must be a just war: that is, a war in which the innocent are defended, suffering is reduced, and there is discrimination between combatants and non-combatants. This second point of view, which holds that although Jesus teaches and gives peace, governments must go to war to protect the innocent, is derived from natural law theory.[51]

Although the letter does not make it clear how a person or a church can hold these two conflicting points of view, the bishops do make it clear that both perspectives are confronted with a unique challenge by the escalation of nuclear arms. Nuclear weapons raise new moral questions. First, the possibility of destruction without limit requires all Christians to refuse to legitimate the idea of nuclear war, for the whole of the just war argument is intended to limit the destructiveness of war. Nuclear war does not discriminate; it magnifies suffering a millionfold; it destroys the innocent. Certainly the mission of America to extend democracy can never be fulfilled by nuclear war.

Second, because nuclear war is morally unjustifiable, the Catholic bishops believe that all Christians must question the political policy of deterrence. A nation has no moral right to threaten what it may never do. In addition, the bishops object to the cost of the policy of deterrence. They quote the statement issued by all the Catholic bishops at Vatican II: "The arms race is one of the greatest curses on the human race and the harm it inflicts upon the poor is more than can be endured."[52]

By inflicting this curse upon the poor of the world, America fails in the first task of its mission, to be an example to the world.

The United Methodist Council of Bishops, in a document entitled *In Defense of Creation: The Nuclear Crisis and a Just Peace,* agrees with the Catholic bishops that Jesus Christ is our peace. They also accept both the pacifist and just war traditions (without resolving the conflicting points of view), and therefore also reject nuclear war and deterrence from the perspective of just war principles. But the United Methodist bishops emphasize that the nuclear crisis must be seen as a matter of social justice as well as a matter of the prevention of war. Christians are called to be peacemakers, to be evangelists of *shalom*—the peace that is overflowing with justice. Therefore, every policy of government must be "an act of justice and must be measured by its impact on the poor, the weak and the oppressed—not only in our own nation, but in all nations."[53] The nuclear arms race offends justice:

> Justice is abused in the overwhelming power of nuclear-weapon states to threaten the self-determination, the security, and the very life of nonaligned and nonbelligerent nations because nuclear hostilities are bound to have devastating environmental and human consequences for the whole earth.
>
> Justice is forsaken in the squandering of wealth . . . in worldwide military spending, while a holocaust of hunger, malnutrition, disease, and violent death is destroying tens of millions of the world's poorest peoples.
>
> Justice is defiled by the superpowers' implication in conventional arms races and proxy wars in the Third World, causing much present suffering and threatening escalation into a nuclear war.
>
> Justice is denied in the increasing concentration and computerization of nuclear decision making so that the people's rights of participation in matters of their own security and survival are nullified.[54]

Both the Catholic and the United Methodist bishops argue directly against the crusade language. They point out that the root of our problem in negotiating disarmament agreements is our way of looking at our relations with the Soviet Union and the world at large. We must avoid the trap of seeing the world only through the anticommunist lens of the evangelical mission of America. "The Soviet people and their leaders are human beings created in the image and likeness of God. To believe we are condemned in the future only to what has been the past of U.S.–Soviet relations is to underestimate both our human potential for creative diplomacy and God's action in our midst."[55]

The point of view expressed by the Catholic and United Methodist bishops brings just war advocates and those who advocate nonviolent resistance close together on the issue of nuclear war. Both groups believe that nuclear war is morally unjustifiable. Both recognize that nuclear weapons are a justice issue. Both groups oppose the language of the crusade in which the wars of America have been justified. Both argue that we must understand anew the human potential for creative diplomacy and God's action in our midst. Both agree that Christians must refuse to participate in nuclear warfare, whether in the production of weapons or the launching of weapons. The powerful and effective crusade images of the evangelical mission of America must be resisted by both nonviolent resisters and just war advocates. Therefore, both groups can join the Catholic bishops in their affirmation:

> As citizens we wish to affirm our loyalty to our country and its ideals, yet we are also citizens of the world who must be faithful to the universal principles proclaimed by the Church. While some other countries also possess nuclear weapons, we may not forget that the United States was the first to build and to use them. Like the Soviet Union, this country now possesses so many weapons as to imperil the continuation of civilization. Americans share responsibility for the current situation, and cannot evade responsibility for trying to resolve it.[56]

Conclusion

The story of the mission of America is a story of the conflict of the exemplary and evangelical themes. The exemplary theme of the mission of America gave birth to and nourished the tradition of democratic reform. That tradition invoked biblical and Enlightenment themes, and motivated Americans to labor together for the sake of a better community. In so doing, Americans lived in a story that mitigated the loneliness and isolation of the individualism of the story of success and the story of well-being.

But the evangelical theme of the mission of America displays the demonic side of the language of community. In his *Moral Man and Immoral Society,* Reinhold Niebuhr notes that there is an ethical paradox in patriotism. Patriotism transmutes individual unselfishness into national egoism, for the individual, giving freely of self for the sake of the larger whole, also gives the nation carte blanche to use the power for any purpose it desires.[57] The evangelical theme of the mission of America baptizes as good all purposes of the American nation, including America's wars and the nuclear arms race.

In reflecting on the biblical story, we noted that a fusion and confusion of stories is commonplace to the human experience. The evangelical mission of America story has been both fused and confused with the biblical story across the history of the nation. One of the reasons for the confusion is that from the beginning of America, through the Civil War and the World Wars, the nation has taken the place of the church for many persons who think with the biblical story. When Christians, who ought to have some other story to rely on to judge the actions of the nation, live in the story of the mission of America as fully as do those who do not think with the biblical story, it is little surprise that the nation is caught in the snares of self-deceit. The evangelical theme of the mission of America has no resources to deal with self-deception. It has become instead the primary cover story for America's relationships with other nations.

If we are to discern the truth of the relationship between America and other nations, we, like the bishops, must find another story in which to live. They remind us that biblical story calls us to live in the peace that Jesus taught and of which his resurrection is the sign—God's peace, the peace of *shalom,* the positive peace of justice, health, and wholeness. Biblical story tells of an alternative community—an alternative to the idolatries, oppressions, and violence that mark the way of the nations. The story of that community speaks of swords turned into plowshares, of arms converted to food, of a jubilee kingdom, and of peace, goodwill to all.

6

The Outsiders

Biblical story, the Enlightenment story of progress, the story of well-being, and the mission of America story are the dominant cultural narratives in America. However, as was noted in the introduction, these four stories, which the majority have taken up, seem to a minority to be transparently deceptive, either in themselves or in the way the powerful appropriate them. In America much of the opposition to the unjust ways the powerful use the dominant narratives of the culture arises from the oppressed. The exercise of racism and sexism by the majority of Americans continues to deny justice, equality, and freedom to Americans of minority races and to women. Such persons and groups are thereby placed outside the promises of full participation in American society.

In light of the reality of oppression, we need to inquire into the way that oppressed groups respond to the cultural narratives. Because many persons of minority groups both take up some of the basic themes of the major cultural stories and reject others, they are at the same time both outsiders and insiders to American cultural narratives. The unique standpoint of insider-outsider gives minorities and women an unusual ability to perceive the way the cultural narratives are used to justify oppression.

Because outsiders see how the cultural narratives of the majority support an oppressive, unjust social order, they seek to refashion the cultural stories by drawing on their own stories, which they have created out of their religious, historical, and cultural experiences. By turning to their own history to show how each cultural narrative has been used to justify oppression, they intend to reorder the cultural vision of the majority. Such a reordering demonstrates that a true understanding of the cultural narratives allows Americans to envision a nation of true freedom and justice for all.

The restatement of the cultural narratives in ways that are at odds with the stories told by the powerful is a difficult task. The religious traditions have provided outsiders with resources that have enabled them to rise to the challenge. Peter Berger points out that while religious traditions are often used to support oppressive social structures, they may also reveal that before the face of God, social arrangements are nothing but human works, devoid of inherent sanctity. More than that, the structures of a society may be unveiled as structures of oppression that must be overthrown in order for a world of justice and peace to come to birth.[1]

Berger argues, therefore, that religion appears in history both as a world-maintaining and a world-shaking force. Religion is world-maintaining because the dominant stories present the world as fashioned by God, unchangeable, a world to which we must learn to adjust. But those religious stories that are able to unveil "the way it is" as being structures of self-deception become stories of world-shaking force. We can see how this is true in American culture in the way the "outsiders" tell their story.[2]

PART ONE
The Black Struggle for Freedom in America

Vincent Harding believes the narratives of the black religious tradition are world-shaking and world-shaping stories.[3] Because America is still in the making, the definitions of America are in flux. The older, racist images of America are being shaken, and new images are being shaped. The central thrust of the history of black people in

America can be understood in the light of the search for a new America. Harding writes:

> So by its very nature our struggle for freedom has been . . . the struggle for a new America where a new vision of humanity would prevail, and Black religion, as many of us realize, has always been central to that struggle for freedom, for a transformed America.[4]

The struggle for a new vision of humanity, for freedom, and for a transformed America is at the same time a struggle against racism.

Racism is an affirmation concerning the fundamental nature of human beings. According to George Kelsey, racism is a declaration of faith that "affirms that the in-race is glorious and pure as to its being, and out-races are defective and depraved as to their being." Such an affirmation divides human beings as human beings. While the racist rejection invariably comes to expression in the institutions of society, the rejection is not fundamentally political or economic in nature. The racist division in the order of human being is a faith commitment. Racism is therefore one of the most powerful forms of self-deception. It becomes a religion in itself, competes for the loyalty of its subjects, and seeks to mold the actions of its adherents to its own vision of self and world.[5]

From the perspective of Peter J. Paris, however, even though black Americans fully oppose white Americans on the issue of racism, in many other ways blacks give uncritical support to much that is typically American. Paris sees this sharing of the common American vision of self and world in terms of what Du Bois called a "double consciousness" on the part of blacks. On one hand, blacks are extremely critical of the racist American way of life; on the other hand, they have a typically American, prereflective, noncritical acceptance of other aspects of the American way of life. Inasmuch as blacks accept noncritically the nonracist aspects of the American cultural narratives, they also participate in the self-deceptions that those narratives engender.

Double consciousness appears primarily in the dual loyalties that black Americans have to the nation and to the race. These loyalties conflict because blacks feel a moral obligation to both nation and race in spite of the moral conflict between them.[6] The classic expression of this dilemma is that of W. E. B. Du Bois:

> It is a peculiar sensation, this double-consciousness. . . . One ever feels his twoness,—an American, a Negro. . . .
> The history of the American Negro is the history of this strife . . . he wishes neither of the older selves to be lost. . . . He simply wishes to make it possible for a man to be both a Negro and an American, without being cursed and spit upon by his fellows, without having the doors of Opportunity closed roughly in his face.[7]

Du Bois concluded that "from this double life every American Negro must live, as a Negro and as an America."[8]

This double consciousness changes the way the four cultural narratives are heard. The understanding of self and world for blacks is thus both like and unlike the white perception. The cultural narratives are still taken up by blacks, but they are translated. The main theme of biblical story becomes one in which God is active on behalf of the oppressed, judges the white oppressor, and rescues the people from bondage. The story of success is pressed into the service of the black community and told as a story by which the race can be uplifted. The celebrity functions of the story of well-being are used in the struggle against racism, and the story of the mission of America undergoes a radical revision in black hands.

Radicalism and Resistance in the Nineteenth Century

American slavery, which John Wesley referred to as "the vilest that ever saw the sun," was the first and principal institution fashioned by the religion of racism in the New World.[9] The primary struggle against slavery was rooted in the black interpretation of the biblical story. Blacks drew on the resources of black religion to carry on the struggle against racism in three ways. Radicalism was the first response. The radical struggle directly opposed racism by armed rebellion or the creation of all-black social structures. The relationship between radicalism and biblical story is perhaps most clearly seen in (1) the fact that Gabriel Prosser, Denmark Vesey, and Nat Turner, the leaders of the largest slave uprisings, all believed that God had called them to the work of freedom, and (2) the first all-black social institution was the Free African Society, which became the African Methodist Church, founded by Richard Allen in 1787.[10]

Radicalism: Nat Turner and David Walker

Of the early black radicals, Nat Turner is the one in whom we most clearly see how biblical story was interpreted by blacks in terms of their freedom struggle. He was born in Virginia in 1800, a year after his mother, Nancy, was captured and sold into slavery. Drawing upon her African traditions, Nancy taught Nat that he had been born to lead his people. His father, by escaping from bondage, taught him that slavery was not to be endured. Nat learned to read the scriptures and heard the Spirit call him to seek first the kingdom of God, a kingdom in which the power of the slave masters would be broken and God's righteousness established on earth. The Spirit assured Nat that God would use him in preparing the way for the righteous kingdom. He was to await God's sign. God's sign would be a signal to Turner that the blacks should arise, destroy the slaveholders, and wait in righteousness for the coming of Christ. So Nat worked, married, preached, prayed, and listened to the voice of the Spirit.[11]

An eclipse of the sun in February 1831 was interpreted by many, black and white alike, as a sign that Christ was soon to return. Nat, however, saw it as the sign of which the Spirit had spoken. He selected four lieutenants and revealed to them his calling. On Saturday, August 13, 1831, the sun grew dim, and a black spot moved across its surface. Nat told the four that the day of judgment was at hand, and God was calling them to cleanse the land of unrighteousness.

Shaped by his immersion in the holy-war tradition of Joshua, Judges, and Ezekiel, Nat intended to prepare for the day of God by putting all slave owners to the sword. Relying on surprise, Nat's band struck down family after family on the road to the county seat, Jerusalem. Nat planned to capture Jerusalem's cache of arms, destroy the city, and wait, like the prophetic warriors of old, for the next word from the Spirit. But news of the rebellion quickly spread, the militia intercepted Nat's band, and the blacks were decisively defeated. None but Nat escaped. After six weeks in hiding, Nat was himself discovered, arrested, tried, and executed.

At one level, Nat Turner was living out the common nineteenth-century interpretation of biblical story. Like thousands of other religious persons, Nat expected the immediate return of Christ to earth and interpreted heavenly phenomena in light of that expectation. But what set Nat apart from the white version of the biblical story was his own experience of slavery and his conviction that God intended to bring slavery to an end. Therefore, Nat Turner envisioned an America that was indeed called of God, but the character of the call was like the call of Israel that Amos heard:

> You alone of all the families of earth, have I acknowledged, therefore it is for all your sins that I mean to punish you.
>
> Amos 3:2

Nat Turner agreed with those Americans who saw America as exceptional, as a sign to the world. But he interpreted the sign by the prophecy of Amos, and agreed with Winthrop that by failing to fulfill God's covenant, America had become a "hissing and byword" among the peoples.

In his *Appeal to the Colored Citizens of the World,* issued in 1829, David Walker arrived at conclusions not far from those of Nat Turner. Walker, a faithful member of a black Methodist church in Boston, was convinced that God had called him to write the *Appeal* and to publish it widely among blacks in America. The publication of the *Appeal* was an act of great courage. A group of Georgia men put a price of $1,000 on Walker's head and vowed they would murder him. When Walker was suddenly afflicted and fell dead in a doorway near his shop in Boston, blacks in Boston were convinced that he had been poisoned.

In the *Appeal,* Walker passionately argues that Africans in the United States are profoundly degraded because of white racism and its economic exploitation, but God is a God of justice who will punish white America by fighting on the side of blacks against the slave owners and by bringing destruction upon the oppressors. God will cause them "to rise up against one another, to be split and divided, and to oppress each other, and sometimes to open hostilities with sword in hand."[12] The responsibilities of black people are to resist oppression in every way, including armed struggle; to develop a profound sense of solidarity among themselves, wherever they live; to become as educated as possible; and to ground the black struggle for justice in the Christian faith. In conclusion, Walker states that it is probably too late to avoid God's fierce wrath, but if America hears God's call to repent, and turns from its racism, there is still a small hope that God will bring a new society of peace and justice into being.[13]

Walker's years of reading, travel, and reflection on the character of white racism enabled him to see clearly the economic motives behind white oppression. He understood, in a way that Nat Turner did not, the full range of the powers that would be mustered against any slave rebellion. But in spite of their very different experiences, both Walker and Turner took up the biblical story that had been handed down to them by white Americans. They read out of that story a vision of self and world that was radically different from that of the white perspective.

Walker and Turner pitted the truth of biblical story against the self-deceptive distortion of the racists. They argued that a human being was created in the image of God, and that God's spirit is the crucial constituent of a human being. Thus all human beings must be treated justly. In their understanding, the hatred and injustice with which whites treated blacks was nothing less than rebellion against God. God had given white Americans a great deal: first of all the gospel, then a good land, overflowing with milk and honey, and finally the opportunity to treat an oppressed and poverty-stricken people with the love with which God had loved them. Instead they had continued the cruelest slave system known to history. Therefore God was coming as judge. The "Day of the Lord" would be the day that Amos imagined, a day of gloom, of darkness, and of judgment. Walker thought that if ever the world might truly follow Christ, and so turn away the day of judgment, it would "be through the means, under God, of the Blacks, who are now held in wretchedness and degradation by the white Christians of the world."[14]

Resistance

A second way in which blacks resisted racism was based on a reinterpretation of both the biblical story and the Enlightenment story of progress. Blacks engaged in resistance by urging Americans to live up to both Christian and revolutionary ideals. In 1774, as soon as British colonists began to claim their rights had been violated by England, blacks petitioned the governor of Massachusetts to grant them freedom. They argued that they, too, were

> a freeborn Pepel and have never forfeited this Blessing by aney compact or agreement whatever. . . . There is a great number of us sencear . . . members of the Church of Christ[. H]ow can the master . . . be said to fulfill that command Live in love let Brotherly Love contuner . . . when he Beares me down with the [heavy] chanes of slavery and operson against my will?[15]

This theme was stated again and again by Frederick Douglass and the many black leaders who shared leadership in the Black Convention movement and the antislavery societies before the Civil War.[16]

The Civil War brought an end to the institution of slav-

ery and a brief opportunity, at least in the South, to create
a new, more just society. Black churches were the organizing bases for the struggle; black preachers were consistently
among the key political leaders in Reconstruction. The
black leadership of that period envisioned a society that
would engage the gifts, talents, and work of all its people
for the common good. The right to vote was considered
sine qua non for the achievement of all other rights and for
the progress of black people.

Henry M. Turner exemplified the black leaders who
made the theme of black liberation the center of both
religion and politics. Turner, who later become one of the
bishops of the African Methodist Episcopal Church, was
elected to the Georgia legislature under the Reconstruction Act of 1867. But as soon as Georgia adopted its
constitution, the legislature ousted its black members.
Turner's expulsion was a sign that racial hatred was not
abating, but shifting its outward expression. Lynching,
segregation, black code laws, and the rise of the Ku Klux
Klan led blacks to rethink the possibility of freedom in
America.[17]

In the bitterness and terror of the post-Reconstruction
years, perhaps the most difficult task was that of maintaining the hope that the talents and gifts of black people
would one day be employed to fashion a new America. The
Reverend Francis J. Grimké, a graduate of Princeton
Theological Seminary and pastor of the 15th Street Pres-
byterian Church in Washington, D.C., is an excellent example of how black pastors drew upon biblical story to
enable their people to hold on to their hope, their understanding of God, and their sense of themselves.[18]

Grimké preached a series of sermons on lynching in
1899. Between 1889 and 1899, 1,204 black men and
women were lynched in the United States. Grimké was
especially angered that local whites celebrated lynchings as
festive occasions. Grimké asked the obvious question:
"How could people, who claimed to be Christian . . . do
such things? How could the American Church . . . permit
this awful, black record of murder and lawlessness?"[19]

Grimké, angered as he was with white American Christianity, still hoped that America would hear the gospel:

> In spite of the shallowness and emptiness and glaring hypocrisy . . . of the church . . . I still believe that Christianity is in this land. Today it is like a little grain of mustard seed . . . like the little lump of leaven which the woman hid in three measures of meal: but it has begun to work, and will go on working, diffusing itself, until the whole is leavened . . . Christianity shall one day have sway even in Negro-hating America. . . . Jesus Christ is yet to reign in this land. I will not see it, you will not see it, but it is coming all the same.[20]

For Grimké, black Christians were the grain of mustard seed planted in American soil, the leaven in the meal that was working itself out until even Negro-hating America should turn to the gospel of Jesus Christ. It was this sense of having been given a divine destiny that gave Grimké and millions of other black American Christians the courage to go on toward freedom. The black church was the arena in which this calling could be exercised, the place where the true story of black and white could be told, and a community in which a true sense of self and world could be fashioned by a biblical story not distorted by racism. The courage to resist racism in the larger society was nurtured by the truthful telling of biblical story within the black church.

Survival

The third response was that of survival. Because racism was most fully manifested in slavery, which dehumanized and often destroyed African Americans, Harding notes that during slavery "the mainstream of the struggle was often given over to the simple fight for survival . . . remaining alive; maintaining sanity, strength and inner dignity regardless of outer poses; carrying children toward the future."[21]

Although many persons, such as Grimké and Du Bois, and many of the official assemblies of the black denominations advocated aggressive action in behalf of civil and political rights, other black leaders advocated a survivalist response to racist laws, customs, and practices in the period following the Civil War. This response came to be known as "accommodationism," and its best-known advocate was Booker T. Washington.[22] Washington did not cast his discussion of the black quest for freedom in the language of biblical story. Washington used the language of the story of success to stress duties rather than rights, industriousness rather than justice, and economic progress rather than politics that reflected a God-given equality. He argued that because such an attitude made a good fit with the labor needs of the expanding commercial and industrial economy of the South, it enhanced the survival of black people. The survivalist response therefore became a black rewrite of the story of success in America.[23]

Radicalism and Resistance in the Twentieth Century

By the turn of the twentieth century the struggle of black Americans against racism and for freedom had developed a history of its own. According to Albert Raboteau, the tradition of black protest challenged the adequacy of the dominant mission-of-America image in four distinct but related ways.[24]

First, black leaders argued that slavery and discrimination were major roadblocks on the road to the fulfillment of America's destiny. Racism, institutionalized in slavery and segregation, made it impossible for America to achieve her destiny as a people who govern themselves in freedom and justice. For many blacks, the American experiment was therefore a failure.

Second, blacks perceived that black Christians were the true exemplars of Christianity in America. The lives of most whites were predominantly shaped by the story of racism rather than the story of Christ. Blacks compared their experience in America to the experience of Israel in Egypt. Such a symbolization opposed the white image of America as God's new Israel and suggested that America was much more conformed to the image of Egypt, the land of bondage under the false god Pharaoh. This criticism stressed that America was not only racist but was so self-deceived in its racism that it did not even recognize its own character.

Third, all across the nineteenth century blacks asserted that because of racism America was failing in its mission to be a "city on a hill," a light and hope to all peoples. But black prophets still continued to hope that America would become a light to the nations. In this hope they urged America to repent and to imitate the Christlike virtues of the black people who suffer in her midst.

Finally, some blacks believed that it was too late. They argued that America's self-deception was too firmly entrenched, that racism had irrevocably formed her character. The "last, best hope" of Western civilization had proved false. For some, like Nat Turner, "too late" meant that the day of the Lord was at hand. For others, "too late" meant that it was time for black people to leave America, to establish their own new nation in Africa. White Christians had failed to be Christian. Other peoples must now take up the gospel of faith and freedom that white Americans had only managed to preach. In these four ways, then, the vision of self and world that emerged from the black experience in America was radically different from that of other Americans.

Gayraud Wilmore has argued that as the black church became more and more accommodated to the culture throughout the first half of the twentieth century, black radicalism disappeared from the churches. The black church emphasized Washington's version of the story of success at the expense of its more radical interpretation of biblical story. Outside the church, however, an alternative form of radical black leadership began to develop.[25]

Radicalism

Marcus Garvey was the best known of such leaders in the first half of the twentieth century. Garvey, a native of

Jamaica, founded the United Negro Improvement Association in 1914. The UNIA was a political, religious, social, recreational, cultural, and economic institution. He organized a division of UNIA in New York City and by 1919 claimed a membership of more than two million. It was the largest and most successful mass movement of urban blacks in the history of the United States.

Garvey mounted a tough, accusatory attack upon all who oppressed blacks. He outlined the sins of whites against blacks: lynching, peonage, disenfranchisement, serfdom, industrial and political inequality, and racial exploitation. He argued that blacks themselves must bring such crimes to an end by establishing a free African nation that would be "strong enough to lend protection to the members of our race scattered all over the world, and to compel the respect of the nations and races of the earth."[26]

Garvey combined this attack on present-day America and his future hope of a free Africa with the practical, day-to-day work of organizing a chain of groceries, restaurants, laundries, a hotel, a doll factory, a printing plant, and a steamship line. He preached ambition, for "to be ambitious is to be great in mind and soul. To want that which is worth while and strive for it."[27] He encouraged blacks to establish and support black businesses. He sought to make daily life better in the ghetto by providing a wide range of social services through UNIA. Thus the UNIA not only attacked the injustice of racism but summoned blacks to self-improvement and humanitarian service.

The UNIA appealed to those who were disappointed with traditional Christianity, imprisoned in the poverty and despair of the ghetto, bitter toward the rising black middle class and its self-righteous success ethic, and angry with American racism. Responding to those who despaired of achieving justice for blacks in America, Garvey spoke of establishing a new Republic of Africa on the ideals that America had betrayed. The hymns, services, catechisms, creeds, and baptismal ceremonies of the UNIA offered blacks a religious cultural nationalism of their own, freed of the ambivalences and betrayals that characterized the American civil religion.

Thus Garvey created for blacks a new black civic religion, a faith in a nation not yet established.[28]

A second stream, not entirely apart from the churches but more secularized and more intellectual, rose in support of Du Bois, the National Association for the Advancement of Colored People (NAACP), and the social radicals such as A. Philip Randolph. This stream drew support from the continuing development of black culture in music, art, and literature. This movement refashioned the cultural stories from the perspective of an intellectual radicalism.

A third stream turned away from the religious and political arenas. Wilmore suggests that this form of radicalism was a belligerent and thoroughly secularized black racism, characterized by bitter reversal of the white racist story. Its home ground was the sporting and criminal elements of Harlem and other northern ghettos. Some of the young men and women from this stream were captured by the vision of the Islamic cults and sects, which nourished their sense of anger and resentment. The best known of the persons who moved from cynicism and hatred to a passionate vision of justice and brotherhood is Malcolm X.[29]

Malcolm was converted to the Black Muslim faith while in prison. In his *Autobiography,* he recited in detail his life at "the very bottom of the American white man's society" in order to show how the power of Allah completely transformed his life. The transformation began with Malcolm's passionate espousal of the Black Muslim teachings and continued in his swift rise from illiterate petty criminal to a self-educated social critic and Islamic prophet of wide-ranging intellect. He claimed that "my alma mater was books, a good library." In prison he studied fifteen hours a day. Out of prison, his extraordinary gifts of intellect and speaking ability soon made him a major spokesman for the Black Muslims.[30]

Malcolm stirred his audiences by inverting the claim that America is a special nation. Malcolm claimed that America was indeed exceptional—it was Satan. He argued that the collective white American's record of cruelties, evils, and greeds were devilish actions directly responsible for both the presence and condition of black people in America. He attacked the hypocrisy of the white Christian religion, which taught love of neighbor but oppressed and exploited blacks. Malcolm's scorn of white racist values was heard gladly in the black communities of the North. As the media transformed Malcolm into a celebrity, his message reached more and more blacks.[31]

Malcolm's rhetoric had more fire than Garvey's, but his political program stood in the same tradition. Malcolm's father had been a Baptist minister who was also a passionate follower of Garvey. Like Garvey, Malcolm argued that blacks wanted human rights and "respect as *human beings!*"[32]

But Malcolm also argued that blacks should focus their efforts toward building and patronizing their own businesses, providing jobs and homes for themselves, and developing black social programs to combat drunkeness, drug addiction, and prostitution in black ghettos. After his pilgrimage to Mecca and his break with the Black Muslims, Malcolm founded a Black Nationalist organization and began to self-consciously develop political, economic, and social philosophies that would "instill within black men the racial dignity, the incentive and the confidence that the black race needs today."[33]

The story of Malcolm X was a story of powerful judgment against the self-deception of white Christianity and against those black churches that did not see or proclaim that self-deception. Malcolm's study of the history of Western civilization convinced him that the white domination of America could not be overcome except by a black community rooted in a different vision of self and world. Western Christianity had become so distorted by the self-deceptions of racism that only through Islam could blacks gain a true understanding of God, self, and world. Both Garvey and Malcolm display the truth of Vincent Harding's observation:

> The search for a new religious pluralism in American society takes place, you see, not only through the churches, but

through other forms of religious organization as well. It surged up out of the cauldron of Black struggle, became the expression of a people in search of a self-definition which would provide integrity and hope for their lives. All of these developments were part of the Black subversion of white religious, political and social domination of America.[34]

King and Nonviolent Resistance to Racism

Martin Luther King, Jr., the son, grandson, and great-grandson of Baptist ministers, enabled the black church to reclaim a radical black interpretation of biblical story. King's commitment to social justice had come early in his life, and he had reflected systematically on social justice and racial oppression in college, seminary, and his Ph.D. program at Boston University. He had read Gandhi's writings on nonviolent resistance to evil. But when he accepted the pastorate of the Dexter Avenue Baptist Church in Montgomery, Alabama, he

> had not the slightest idea that I would later become involved in a crisis in which nonviolent resistance would be applicable. I neither started the protest nor suggested it. I simply responded to the call of the people for a spokesman. When the protest began, my mind, consciously or unconsciously, was driven back to the Sermon on the Mount, with its sublime teachings on love, and the Gandhian method of nonviolent resistance.[35]

As the days unfolded, and blacks refused to ride the buses of Montgomery by day and packed the church meetings by night, King came to understand the power of nonviolence. In his sermons, addresses, articles, and books he reflected upon the daily events and slowly fashioned for himself and the nation an interpretation of biblical story that was rooted in the black experience and stressed nonviolent resistance to evil. Resistance was required because "freedom was never given to anybody," and to accept the system of segregation was "to cooperate with evil." Resistance was required to disrupt the false peace that lay like a thin veneer over the racist practices. The protest was required to be nonviolent, however, because the protesters were not seeking to defeat or humiliate the opponents, but to create "the beloved community." Thus nonviolent action came to signify much more than just "protest." Nonviolent action was an active faith and confidence in the God who was carrying black and white together toward the Promised Land of freedom. It was a form of Christian love, a love for the white man whose soul was scarred and whose personality was greatly distorted by racism.[36]

Across the South, King's leadership enabled black people to create such public tension that whites were required to respond. In Birmingham, Alabama, the white religious leadership responded to King's presence with an attack on the civil rights movement, arguing that the demonstrations were unwise and untimely. King replied with an eloquent defense, "Letter from Birmingham Jail."

In his "Letter," King sought to illuminate the depths of white American self-deception. King hoped that the clergy of Birmingham would ally with him in Christ's cause of justice and love. But most of the ministers said, "Those are social issues, with which the gospel has no real concern." Most churches committed "themselves to a completely otherworldly religion which [made] a strange, unbiblical distinction between body and soul" and which preached a private gospel of well-being.[37]

King argued that demonstrations were rituals of revival for blacks, calling them to participate in their own freedom movement, calling the nation to repent of racism, and forcing whites to choose whether they would serve the God of racism or the God of justice. The movement, by "standing up for what is best in the American dream and the most sacred values in our Judeo-Christian heritage," hoped to redeem the nation and bring it back to those "great wells of democracy which were dug deep by the founding fathers in their formulation of the Constitution and the Declaration of Independence."[38] King argued:

> We will reach the goal of freedom in Birmingham and all over the nation, because the goal of America is freedom.

Abused and scorned though we may be, our destiny is tied up with America's destiny. Before the pilgrims landed at Plymouth, we were here. Before the pen of Jefferson etched the majestic words of the Declaration of Independence across the pages of history, we were here. . . . If the inexpressible cruelties of slavery could not stop us, the opposition we now face will surely fail. We will win our freedom because the sacred heritage of our nation and the eternal will of God are embodied in our echoing demands.[39]

King's radical Christian retelling of the story of racism displays the reality of America's self-deception. According to Stephen Oates, an essential part of King's storytelling art was his use of public drama. King was an imaginative artist who knew how to fashion a demonstration into a dramatic production that gripped not only the actors on the scene, but the millions who participated via television. The drama forced white Americans to face the distance between their idealized image of America and the bitter reality in which blacks lived. If they wished to be on the side of democracy, of justice, and of love, they needed to join the cause of blacks.[40]

The logic of King's reflection on biblical story carried him beyond the single cause of blacks in America. The vision of "the beloved community" embraced the world, and especially the world of Vietnam. King had, from the beginning of the movement, connected the determination of American blacks to win freedom from oppression with the same longing that motivates oppressed persons everywhere. But America's involvement in the Vietnam War was placing the full power of the nation on the wrong side of the struggle against injustice and poverty. America was exercising "power without compassion, might without morality, and strength without sight."[41]

At home, King's concern about the relationship between racism and economic injustice had led him to organize the "Poor People's Campaign," a nonviolent action crusade that meant to attack economic injustices on behalf of all the poor. The war had diverted billions of dollars from programs such as Head Start, job retraining, public works, and low-income housing. The poor, however, carried more than a fair share of the economic burden of the war. While the children of the upper and middle classes received college deferments, the children of the poor went, in unusually high proportion, to fight in Vietnam.[42]

King argued that everyone dedicated to peace and justice must speak to America in the name of the aliens, the enemies, the poor, and the oppressed. Every nation, America included, needed to develop an overriding loyalty to humanity as a whole. "Now let us begin," King proclaimed at Riverside Cathedral in New York City. "Now let us rededicate ourselves to the long and bitter—but beautiful—struggle for a new world. The choice is ours, and though we might prefer it otherwise we must choose in this crucial moment of human history."[43]

Conclusion

In Martin Luther King, Jr., and the black freedom movement that surged around him, argued with him, denounced him, loved him, and mourned him, the questions about the mission of America were raised with great intensity and with great impact upon the nation as a whole. The questions were the fundamental ones: What is America? What is America's past, culture, public religion? Who is included and who is excluded? Is there still hope that America might be America?

Through the powerful medium of nonviolent direct action, King dramatically intensified the four basic challenges to the mission of America that blacks had been articulating since the nineteenth century. First, the movement demonstrated with new urgency and power that racism, institutionalized in segregation and discrimination, made it impossible for America to achieve her destiny as a people of freedom and justice. Second, black people, who were willing to take up nonviolent resistance to evil, were the true exemplars of Christianity. They were the people who were willing to love neighbor as self, to turn the other cheek, and to seek to redeem even their enemies. Third, if

America was to become a city on the hill, a light to all peoples, white America needed to repent of its racist religion and to make its cause one with the cause of the nonviolent black people in its midst. King's dramatic reenactment of the challenge to America was an affirmation of the hopes of millions: "I have a dream that one day this nation will rise up and live out the true meaning of its creed: 'We hold these truths to be self-evident; that all men are created equal.' "[44] Fourth, as the sixties progressed, King warned that it might soon be too late for America to make changes. Without the basic building blocks of good schools and good jobs, the ghettos were filling with those who did not know how to create good lives or how to participate in building a good society. If America is to be a land of freedom and equality for all, King argued, Americans must deal with racism, poverty, and injustice. Otherwise the hope will die that America will ever be America.

As Harding has suggested, if America is to be America, the experience of black people must be used as a resource for the renewal of the whole society. First of all, black people have learned through their experience with racism that the cultural narratives of the powerful have been full of self-deception and have supported unjust social structures. That is why it is so dangerous to put one's future in someone else's hands. In the 1988 presidential primary campaign, Jesse Jackson sounded that warning again and again as he argued that blacks, women, farmers, workers, and all disadvantaged people needed to participate more fully in the political process, to find "common ground" on which to stand so they could take responsibility for their own future.

Second, the black freedom struggle also demonstrated that only a religious community was able to survive oppression and still continue to hope. In his speech to the Democratic National Convention, Jackson reminded his hearers of the defeats suffered by blacks in the 1964 convention. Many had died in the struggle for freedom in Mississippi, and hundreds were beaten and jailed. Nevertheless, the racist delegation from Mississippi was accepted, and the Mississippi Freedom Democratic party delegation was rejected. But black people had not given up hope. They continued to work. In 1988, a black man headed the Mississippi delegation, and the party was integrated. The black religious community had been able to reach out beyond itself, reach out in compassion to its oppressors, reach out beyond the religion of its oppressors, and catch up "all of the great human experiences of scattering, of defeat, of trial and tribulation, of hope and ecstasy."[45]

It is this catching up of the great human experiences that makes the black religious community so valuable to the majority white community in America. Through the black experience, whites can gain a new insight into their own understanding of self and world. That insight can enable Americans to understand more clearly the nonwhite oppressed majority of the world. The experience of oppression and suffering at the hands of white America enables blacks to see more clearly and speak more truthfully of the oppression and suffering that the mission of America brought to the world.[46]

PART TWO
Women's Struggle for Equality

Sexism—the subjugation of women to men—arose in an early period in human history, excluded women from equal development in the more valued spheres of culture, and became part of the ideology of historical civilizations. The primary stories of American culture, including the biblical story, have been shaped by sexism. Since these stories fashioned the individual and cultural understandings of self and world, they in turn made sexism appear to be the normative nature of human relations. Like the story of racism, the story of sexism gave shape to the culture because (1) it was the story of the male ruling class, (2) its ongoing presence gave it a self-legitimating power, and (3) it had become in some way commensurate with the experience and imagination of the majority of ordinary people.[47]

From the founding of the American colonies, however, some women were convinced that sexism created a world of oppression for women. They therefore sought to restate the cultural narratives. But since the cultural narratives presented the sexist world as a world fashioned by God or nature, women who revisioned the world were branded as heretics or witches. The "world maintaining" aspect of the religious tradition proved to be a powerful support for the sexist worldview.[48]

However, the religious tradition also provided a resource for women to draw upon to resist subjugation. In early America, men used biblical story as their authority to assign women to the role of "helpmeet." Some women argued, however, on the grounds of biblical story itself, that there ought to be no subjugation of women to men among Christians. In the nineteenth century, men developed the doctrine of "woman's sphere" as the corollary of the story of success. But some women argued, on the grounds of both biblical story and the story of progress, that women were created equal to men and were endowed by their Creator with the same inalienable rights. In the twentieth century, men envisioned the world of romantic sexuality as the world in which women were to take up the pursuit of their own well-being. But some women affirmed, on the basis of biblical story and the story of well-being, that the image of "woman as person" must take center stage if there is to be an end to the oppression of women.[49]

Finally, because each of the cultural narratives still strongly supports sexism, contemporary scholars continue to deepen the feminist critique. Therefore, to more fully understand how women imagine themselves in our culture, we need to comment on both the historical and the contemporary critiques of the sexist images in each cultural narrative.

Cover Stories: Helpmeet, Woman's Sphere, Romancer

Each cultural narrative tells a story about the "good woman." Because the stories about the good woman are told in order to sustain the self-interest of the dominant males, they are cover stories. They justify the subjugation of women to men. The good woman is a helpmeet, or keeps to woman's sphere, or fulfills the needs of a man for romantic sexuality. A brief examination of each of these cover stories and the critiques of these stories by women will enable us to more fully understand both the pervasiveness of sexism in American culture and the continuing struggle of women for equality.

The Helpmeet

Early Americans fashioned several images of womanhood out of the mix of religious visions, regions, and classes that composed the colonies. The fullest descriptions of the colonial ideals of womanhood have come from the Puritans, the most literate of the colonists. The primary way in which woman was storied in Puritan America was in terms of "helpmeet": that is, the God-given partner in the colonial family economy. The helpmeet was often referred to as "Adam's rib." In a wedding sermon, a Puritan preacher outlined the place of the helpmeet: "Our ribs were not ordained to be our rulers. They are not made of the head to claim superiority, but out of the side to be content with equality." The good man was to treat his wife as his yoke-fellow or helpmeet; the good woman was always to hold her husband in reverence "as her head in all things."[50]

The "equality" with which the helpmeet was to be content was an equality of work, not an equality of status. Most social and economic life took place within the colonial household. Women were adept in dairying, marketing, spinning, sewing, preserving, and bartering. But the home was much more than the center of economic production. The New England wife bore an average of eight children and was responsible for their discipline, education, and piety. In addition, town officers sent widows, orphans, and the poor into respectable homes for care. Likewise, the church depended upon the women of the congregation to visit the sick, care for the poor, support the bereaved, and so bind the church into a true family of God. Even though women carried responsibility for the public good, were partners in the economic enterprise, and were companions in marriage, they were still denied the right to vote, to speak on public issues, to teach or preach in the church, to own property, or to be tried before peers. The story of a helpmeet as one who was content with "equality" was clearly a cover story.[51]

Although many colonial women probably accepted subordination, the Puritan story of helpmeet was challenged from the founding of the colony because a considerable number of women applied the implications of Paul's teachings to themselves. The themes of equality in Galatians, the sanctioning of women as teachers in Titus, and the recognition of the ancient biblical tradition of women as prophets in Corinthians all underlined the contradiction between the Puritan understanding of helpmeet and a more truthful interpretation of biblical story.[52]

By 1637, Ann Hutchinson was applying the teachings of Paul in a positive way to her own life and ministry. She argued that according to Paul, she could teach in her own house; that she, as an older woman like those to whom Paul referred, had a ministry of teaching younger women; that, like Priscilla, she was called to teach men when so asked; and above all, because she had been given the gift of prophecy, she was called of God to use it under "the rule of the new creature . . . there is neither male nor female, for you are all one in Christ Jesus." Compelled by these convictions, she began to hold meetings in her home. Her ministry of preaching was like "a summons out of the wilderness" to the women of Boston, and they were drawn in large numbers to her house on High Street. Hutchinson's bold and radical proposition that spiritual equality before God sanctioned social equality of men and women on earth soon attracted men as well as women to her preaching. She ignited a controversy that wreaked havoc in Boston, embarrassed its governor, and resulted in a trial that condemned her for behavior that was considered neither "tolerable nor comely in the sight of God nor fitting for your sex."[53]

Quaker women were also at the forefront of re-visioning the story of helpmeet. Both George Fox and Margaret Fell, the founders of the Religious Society of Friends (Quakers), championed equality for women and encouraged their ministries. Their doctrines of spiritual rebirth, direct inspiration by the Divine Light, and the legitimacy of lay ministries were important to women. They argued that the Puritan requirement that women be silent in the church did not apply to those in whom the spirit of Christ dwelled. Thus of the first fifty-nine Quaker evangelists to come to America, twenty-six were women. Mary Dyer, challenged by the example of Anne Hutchinson and inspired by the inner light, taught publicly in Boston. She was twice arrested, convicted, and banished from the Massachusetts Bay Colony. Upon her third return to the colony, she was arrested and hanged for speaking in public.[54]

The second Great Awakening provided a larger opportunity for women to reinterpret the biblical story and thereby create a role of genuine equality. About two thirds of the persons active in the revivals were women. They testified in public to the power of the Spirit in their lives, led public prayer groups, and became the principal local organizers for the great evangelists such as Charles Finney. In the face of considerable hostility, women began to speak and pray before groups composed of both men and women. The practice spread. By 1850, women such as Phoebe Palmer began to do revival preaching in those churches that placed great stress on the gifts of the Spirit. Many women who heard Palmer preach, such as Frances Willard and Catherine Booth, were called to public ministry. Booth, who with her husband, William, founded the Salvation Army, was an outstanding revival preacher. Willard served as an evangelist with Dwight Moody and as president of the Women's Christian Temperance Union. Both argued for the equality of women in ministry and in marriage. Through such efforts women transformed the theology of the Great Awakenings into a theology of liberation and dismantled the cover story of helpmeet.

The nineteenth-century re-visioning of biblical story was crowned by the issuing of *The Woman's Bible* in 1895. Elizabeth Cady Stanton, who initiated the project, argued that a version of the Bible that collected and interpreted all statements referring to women in the Bible was necessary for two reasons: (1) The Bible was constantly used as a political weapon against women struggling for their rights, and (2) it was so used because the Bible was written and interpreted by men who never saw or talked with God. Stanton sought to develop a scientific commentary on the passages that speak of women, hoping to break through the crust of male interpretation. But she concluded that the Bible was "man-made": that is, it was written by men, in male language, and was the expression of a patriarchal culture.[55]

The criticism that biblical story is an interpretation by men for the benefit of men is perhaps most clearly made in the present by Elisabeth Schüssler Fiorenza. In her feminist theological reconstruction of Christian origins, *In Memory of Her,* Fiorenza draws upon both the biblical text and the recent scholarly interest in the social world of Christian beginnings to show that women were participatory actors in the early Christian churches. Mark, the earliest Gospel, tells a story of the failure of the male disciples and the faithfulness of the women disciples. All the Gospels agree that women are the first witnesses of the resurrection and that at first the male disciples refuse to believe. Luke emphasizes the fact that women journey with Jesus during his ministry just as male disciples do, and Jesus commends Mary for having chosen the part of the disciple. Likewise, Paul's letters often refer to the leadership of women in the early Christian missionary movement.[56]

Finally, Fiorenza points out that the early Christian movement was attractive to women precisely because Jesus and Paul both stressed egalitarian relationships: Jesus says, "No; anyone who wants to become great among you must be your servant, and anyone who wants to be first among you must be slave to all" (Mark 10:43–44), and Paul teaches that "there are no more distinctions between Jew and Greek, slave and free, male and female, but all of you are one in Christ Jesus" (Gal. 3:28). Therefore, to interpret the life and teachings of Jesus and the structure of the early church from a patriarchal point of view is a clear case of self-deception. To truly understand the Jesus movement and the scriptures that bear witness to it requires the use of a conceptual framework that places women at the center of social relations and political institutions, for the early Christian movement was inclusive of women's leadership.

Woman's Sphere

The nineteenth century witnessed the rise of the cover story "woman's sphere." Woman's sphere was an adaptation of the male story of success. The spread of the democratic faith, which stressed the equal worth of each individual, contributed to the erosion of the Puritan notion of a God-given hierarchy. But as Beverly Harrison has argued, industrialization, which created a new urban middle class, was a significant force in changing the view of women. With this class, a new social ideal of "womanhood" came into being. In radical contrast to colonial women, middle-class urban wives were separated from any economic function. The "good woman" came to be the woman whose world was that of the home and of personal relationships.[57]

Because the story of success had become such an important image of self and world for men in the nineteenth century, women were also urged to succeed. In contrast to men, women were to succeed by exercising the "feminine virtues": purity, piety, love, and compassion. These virtues, considered "natural" to women, were to be exercised in personal rather than public relationships. The feminine virtues had a public effect, however, for the support of a virtuous woman was considered necessary if a man was to succeed in the rough-and-tumble public world of war, work, and politics. Therefore, a woman was to be judged primarily by the character of her relations to her husband and children and by her personal response to those in need of love and compassion. Through this world of personal relationships a woman was to participate in the struggles of the story of success.

Women's virtues, exercised in woman's private sphere, were also seen to have a crucial public effect on the mission of America. Without the concern of women for human ties, the raw rages of men would destroy the morals of the society and place at risk the nation itself. Suffrage advocates faced this argument when they attempted to have the word *sex* included in the Fifteenth Amendment, so that the right to vote could not be denied on account of race, color, *sex*, or previous condition of servitude. Senator Frederick Frelinghuysen of New Jersey drew upon the vision of the mission of America as he told the story of woman's sphere:

> the God of our race has stamped upon [the women of America] a milder, gentler nature, which not only makes them shrink from, but disqualifies them for the turmoil and battle of public life. They have a higher and a holier mission. . . . Their mission is at home, by their blandishments and their love to assuage the passions of men as they come in from the battle of life, and not themselves by joining in the contest to add fuel to the very flames. . . . It will be a sorry day for this country when those vestal fires of love and piety are put out.[58]

In the first half of the nineteenth century, women began to undermine the cover story of woman's sphere. Having learned to exercise leadership in the Second Great Awakening, women undertook reforms in the larger society and thus became involved in issues that were beyond woman's sphere. Women organized themselves into missionary societies, Sunday school associations, infant schools, schools for poor and black children, temperance societies, and the Female Anti-Slavery Society. Women, who still had no political nor economic standing in the community, used these associations to master the procedures of the emerging commercial economy. They collected large sums of money, exercised organizational leadership, and created a major public role for women beyond revivals.[59]

The development of a public role for women in the Great Awakening and the reform associations led to a more direct challenge to the story of woman's sphere. At first, the newly emerging public roles of women were centered in religious institutions, which stressed the virtues of piety, love, and compassion. But under the leadership of two of the most noted women abolitionists, Sarah and Angelina Grimké, the ideology of woman's sphere was directly confronted, and women claimed a public role as full and responsible citizens.

The Grimké sisters were born into a prosperous slaveholding family in South Carolina and turned against the slavery that they had witnessed as children. They moved to Philadelphia and joined the Quakers and the Philadelphia Female Anti-Slavery Society. They began their own abolitionist work with a series of "parlor talks" to women in New York. But soon there were so many women eager to attend that no parlor would hold them, and the pastor of a Baptist church offered them his church. The announcement that women were to lecture in a church was shocking, and many abolitionists opposed the move.[60]

The lectures were so successful, however, that the Grimké sisters were invited to tour the New England area. The meetings grew even larger, and soon men began to attend the lectures. A public controversy arose: Ought women to speak on political issues, and to "mixed audiences," just as men did, or ought women to be silent on political issues and speak only to women, and thus respect woman's sphere? The debate culminated with Angelina Grimké's series of addresses to the Massachusetts Legislature in February 1838. No American woman had ever spoken to a legislative body. Grimké pointed out that she represented the twenty thousand women of Massachusetts who had petitioned the legislature on abolition. But because they were women, who ought to have nothing to do with political controversies, the petitioners were disregarded. Grimké asked:

> Are we aliens, because we are women? Are we bereft of citizenship because we are mothers, wives and daughters of a mighty people? Have women *no* country—*no* interests staked in public weal—no liabilities in common peril—no partnership in a nation's guilt and shame? . . . I hold, Mr. Chairman, that American women have to do with this subject, not only because it is moral and religious, but because it is *political,* inasmuch as we are citizens of this republic and as such our honor, happiness and well-being are bound up in its politics, government and laws.[61]

Other feminists, such as Susan B. Anthony and Elizabeth Cady Stanton, took up the challenge to woman's sphere. They made an impassioned plea for women's suffrage at the Seneca Falls convention in 1848 and campaigned for voting rights for women for the next half century.[62] But voting rights were not the only aspect of woman's sphere they attacked. Stanton was convinced that the code of laws and customs that governed marriage were barbarous. To the 1856 women's rights convention she posed the questions, How can a woman subscribe to a theology that makes her a "conscientious victim of another's will? . . . How can she tolerate customs by which a woman is stripped of true virtue, dignity and nobility?" Since marriage was a man-made institution, inherently unjust to wives, Stanton argued that it ought not to be regulated by either church or state. Instead, marriage ought to be "a contract made by equal parties to lead an equal life, with equal restraints and privileges on either side."[63]

The doctrine of woman's sphere, developed for middle- and upper-class women, did not apply to immigrant and working-class women. Their working conditions in mill, factory, and sweatshop left little room for the development of the gentle character of homemaker prescribed for middle-class women. The ruthlessness of trusts and big business in the late nineteenth century made Carnegie's survival-of-the-fittest image a grim reality for workers. Although working men saw themselves as breadwinners, competing in the times of low wages and erratic employment to be among the fittest who would climb the ladder of success, women workers did not live in either the success of woman's-sphere stories. Working women's stories became stories of bread givers.[64]

The realistic stories of Anzia Yezierska reveal the texture of immigrant Jewish life on New York's Lower East Side at the turn of the century. *Bread Givers,* like Yezierska's other novels, immediately plunges the reader into the woman's experience of immigration. Women struggle to provide just the basic necessities for their families and wear themselves out at the task. But one of Yezierska's heroines, wanting more for herself, responds to this bread-giving image of woman by saying of her mother, "I loved her because she gave up so much of herself. But I knew I could never, never be like that."[65]

Bread Givers tells the story of Yezierska herself through the character Sara Smolinsky. Sara's life is an intense conflict between the older images of bread giving and the newer images of well-being. The Smolinskys have immigrated from Russia. Sara's father is a holy man, who keeps the tradition of reading the Torah all the day long and depends upon the work of his wife and four daughters. When he chants the psalms, Sara's mother forgets the lack of boarders, money, or dowries for the daughters. Instead, "Father's holiness filled her eyes with light."[66]

As a growing child, Sara sees the damage done to her sisters by the patriarchal tradition in which her family lives. She is determined to be a modern American woman and to live out the American dream of finding both true love and meaningful work. She drives herself through night school, refuses the husband her father chooses for her, goes on to college, and becomes a teacher. But her father's words ring in her ears: "A woman's highest happiness is to be a man's wife, the mother of a man's children. You're not a person at all. . . . Who ever heard of such madness? You'll rot away by yourself."[67]

More painful than her father's words are the memories of her mother's love. Sara struggles with the dilemma of how to escape her mother's subjection to patriarchy and still affirm her mother's outstanding virtue—a boundless and forgiving love. Although the novel closes with Sara taking her widowed father to her own home, she is not able to do it easily. The role of bread giver is not a joy as it was for her mother, but a "shadow, still there, over me. It wasn't just my father, but the generations who made my father whose weight was still upon me."[68]

Middle-class women reformers who turned their energy toward caring for the large number of those who were exploited, broken, and discarded by the rapid industrialization of America also used the image of bread giving. Jane Addams, founder of Hull House in Chicago, first president of the Women's International League for Peace and Freedom, and winner of the Nobel Peace Prize, was self-consciously a feminist. She advocated women's suffrage and an active role for women in the world. She argued that women needed to move from the arts of pleasing to the development of intellectual force and the capability for the direct employment of that force. Hull House was the incarnation of that argument. Yet she still expressed herself in the images of social housekeeping.

> We still retain the old ideal of womanhood—the saxon lady whose mission it was to give bread unto her household. So we have planned to be 'Breadgivers' throughout our lives, believing that in labor alone is happiness, and that the only true and honorable life is one filled with good works and honest toil, we will strive to idealize our labor and thus happily fulfill woman's noblest mission.[69]

The settlement-house movement was an experimental blend of intellectual effort and direct action. The movement fired the imagination and the intense political involvement of many women. Women learned how to push through labor legislation, to establish juvenile courts, to provide decent schools, to create adequate enforcement of housing and sanitation laws, and to agitate effectively for broader participation of women in politics. They realized that often they were unable to influence elected officials because they had no vote. The suffrage movement itself thus gained strength from the broad concerns of women reformers who at first had seen themselves more as bread givers than as those who would dismantle woman's sphere.[70]

The ratification of the Nineteenth Amendment undermined the ideology of woman's sphere, for it confirmed the right of women to undertake public political action. It was, of course, not the end of the struggle for justice. And the story of two spheres, the one of the family, "a haven in a heartless world," and the other of the competitive world of work, continued to influence the understanding that both men and women had of their work and their family relationships.[71]

Like the story of success for men, the story of woman's sphere promised women that they could control their own lives, because women shaped the "real" world: that is, the world of relationships. The weakness of the story of woman's sphere was its misrepresentation of the power of women. The "separate but equal" sphere of women was separate but never equal, because the ideology of woman's sphere was fashioned by men for the benefit of men.

Jessie Bernard documents the way men benefit and women are at risk in the world of woman's sphere. Married women lose ground in personal development and self-esteem during the early and middle years of adulthood—the same years when men usually show dramatic growth. The housewife suffers more than single or working women from a variety of psychological illnesses. Participation in woman's sphere produces genuine emotional health hazards for women.[72]

On the other hand, the traditional American marriage is very good to most men. Men evidence rapid personal, social, and economic growth. Twice as many married as never-married men report themselves as very happy. Jessie Bernard writes, "There are few findings more consistent, less equivocal, more convincing than the sometimes spectacular and always impressive superiority on almost every index—demographic, psychological, or social—of married over never-married men.[73]

The story of woman's sphere is therefore a cover story. Like the story of success for men, it is destructive for those who are caught up in it. Its images divide men and women, rather than encouraging them to live together in a covenant of mutual support. Since the story argues that women have been placed in their own sphere by their biological nature, there are no resources within the story itself to combat self-deception. The real story of exploitation of women by men is not grasped. Therefore, most men and some women continue to be blind to the reality that the ideology of woman's sphere is oppressive.[74]

Romantic Sexuality: A Woman's Well-being

By the middle twenties, women shared the primary story of American culture: the search for well-being. *Twenty Years in Hull House* gave way to stories of romantic sexuality. Indeed, romantic sexuality became the image of the way to well-being. As in the stories of men, the silver screen chronicled the new image of self and world. In movies such as *True Heart Susie,* Lillian Gish played roles that displayed the fragility of the old ways and the vigor of the new. Susie's old-time values were in conflict with those of the "fast crowd." Susie lost her childhood sweetheart to the flapper Bettina, who flaunted a painted face, short skirts, and sexy walk. The old ways at last triumphed, but not because of their own inherent goodness. Before Susie won her man back, Bettina had displayed vile cooking, a plain unpainted face, and an affair with another man; she then died of pneumonia for good measure. The new strong heroines of the later twenties were the likes of Clara Bow and Joan Crawford, who created and re-created the image of the new woman—zestful, energetic, and fun-loving; one who exuded activism and independence, an active sex partner as well as a buddy. Sociologists thought they could discern a new type of woman evolving, "a woman sophisticated, self-reliant, competent—a woman of the world."[75]

Under the joint impact of film, advertising, and romantic popular literature, the heterosexual relationship came to be seen as the primary arena in which women could achieve success and attain well-being. The heroines in the short stories in women's magazines changed from career women of spirit, courage, and independence to women who were about to become or who already were happy suburban housewives. For them, the resolution of the story was usually either marriage or the birth of yet another child. Women were thus oriented toward competition for men and encouraged to withdraw into a private sphere of heterosexual relations.[76]

Betty Friedan called this orientation "the feminine mystique." The dominance of the feminine mystique was briefly challenged with the expanded work roles for women during World War II. But with the war's end, women returned to their previous role. Women produced more children than they had produced for three generations, and suburbs grew at an astounding rate.[77]

The appeal of the suburbs to women was intimately linked to the image of romantic sexuality as *the* way to well-being for women. The popular press presented the comfort and seclusion of a suburban home as the ideal way to happiness for a woman. In the suburb, a husband and wife could develop a close emotional tie through shared activities (golf, bridge, PTA, and Little League) and express that tie in the privacy of the spacious master bedroom. The flapper was one image of romantic sexuality. The suburban "total woman"—wife, companion, sex partner—was another.

On the other side of private existence in the suburb, however, was loneliness and isolation. Betty Friedan, interviewing her 1942 Smith classmates fifteen years after graduation, discovered that many women had found that the story of romantic sexuality, of the happy wife-mother-companion, was a cover story. The real story was a tale of women trapped on an endless treadmill of dull tasks.[78]

As Friedan defined it, the feminine mystique was the "American dream" of young women:

Their only dream was to be perfect wives and mothers; their highest ambition to have five children and a beautiful house, their only fight to get and keep their husbands. They had no thought for the unfeminine problems of the world outside the home; they wanted the men to make the major decisions.[79]

But Friedan believed that the dream had gone awry. The core of the problem for women was that of identity. The feminine mystique stunted the growth of women. It did not allow women to gratify their basic need to fulfill their potential as human beings. It had always been considered right, Friedan argued, for men to suffer the agonies of the search for their own identities. Indeed, a major theme of American writers had been the search for identity by the young man who "can't go home again." But women were not expected to grow up to find out who they were, to choose their human identity. Because they were women, they were to find their identity through others, either their husbands or their children. According to the feminine mystique, anatomy was woman's destiny; the identity of woman was determined by her biology.[80]

Friedan was certain that once a woman began to recognize the self-deception of the feminine mystique, once she came to realize that neither her husband nor her children nor her homemaking could give her a self, she could readily return to the real story of her life. The real story was that each person must discover the path to self-identity. In our culture, the discovery of creative work of one's own was the way to self-identity, for men and women alike. The work must be work that a woman could take seriously as part of her own life plan; it must be work in which she could grow as part of society.[81]

Woman as Person

By the 1970s, a new image of woman began to emerge in American society. It was an image of woman-as-person—an autonomous, energetic, and competent person, not defined by her household role or responsibilities as wife or mother, and not limited by gender characteristics.[82]

The image of woman-as-person has grown in influence for three reasons. First, millions of women responded to Betty Friedan's revelation of the self-deceptive character of the feminine mystique. Second, women responded to the growing demand for white-collar workers in the service industries, and thus the plausibility of the feminine mystique was undermined.

Third, the civil rights movement provided national leadership in combating discrimination. For a long time even feminists did not perceive that the treatment of women was a civil rights issue. Sexual discrimination was outlawed by the Civil Rights Act before women had established a civil rights–type organization or lobbied for its passage. The new feminist civil rights organization, the National Organization for Women (NOW), was formed in 1966 in response to the complaint of women that the law that made sexual discrimination illegal was not being enforced. NOW used the images and metaphors of the early, more optimistic phase of the civil rights movement to think about women. NOW declared that it was time to confront with concrete action "the conditions which now prevent women from enjoying the equality of opportunity and freedom of choice which is their right as individual Americans and as human beings."[83]

The civil rights movement had a second impact on the images with which women thought about themselves and their world. The drive for school desegregation led to a major examination of stereotypes about black children. The new psychological literature on stereotyping soon began to include sexual stereotyping. The Freudian image of woman as inherently passive was attacked. Other societal attitudes toward women were also criticized. Competition, success, competence, and intellectual achievement were no longer considered to be basically inconsistent with femininity.[84]

The third set of images of woman-as-person arose out of the later conflict-oriented model of the civil rights movement. Liberation became a central theme, and that theme was developed at length in literature such as Kate Millett's *Sexual Politics*. Millett argued that any change in the quality of life for women required the freeing of humanity from the tyranny of patriarchy. NOW took up the new image, departed from consensus politics, and became a conflict-oriented women's liberation organization. It asserted the self-interest and well-being of women as vigorously as possible. A series of controversies arose. Best-sellers such as Gail Sheehy's *Passages* made the argument that family was a zero-sum game, a competitive arena in which there were only winners or losers. Therefore, if a woman's well-being demanded it, divorce was an attractive and vital option.[85]

But abortion was the most heated of the debates. Beverly Wildung Harrison, writing in 1983, argued that the abortion issue centered on the question, "Who shall control the power to reproduce the species?" According to Harrison, patriarchal institutions have enabled men to exercise control over women's reproductive power. Women have needed to gain control over their own lives, in order to reflect on abortion in a "moral context that both affirms and advocates women's well-being." The disvaluation of women has been so deeply embedded in Western culture "that males . . . are inclined to transmit inherited patterns of misogyny unawares." From the moral point of view, therefore, the question that ought to have been asked is, What sort of society must we become if we are to reduce the need for abortion, *and at the same time* increase the quality and range of choice in most women's lives?

Harrison answers the question by suggesting that we need to be the sort of society that embraces every child in a covenant of love and affirmation that begins with the mother and father and extends outward to the wider community. Since we are so far from being such a society, most women choose abortions in situations dominated by desperation, in which it is much easier to say no than yes to the prospective covenant. What women recognize in the present situation, and men do not, is that it is *childbearing,* not abortion, that is the consummately moral action. Because of this radical difference in the way women and men imagine the world, Harrison is not arguing for consensus but for liberation.[86]

But most persons who take up the woman-as-person figure with which to know self and guide action do not speak of well-being in covenantal language as does Harrison. The dominant metaphors with which people think about well-being are therapeutic. In *Habits of the Heart*, Robert Bellah points out that the fundamental character of therapeutic language is that it "enables the individual to think of commitments—from marriage and work to political and religious involvement—as enhancements of the sense of individual well-being rather than as moral imperatives." The central difficulty of such language is that the persons who dwell in it cannot think about themselves or others except as individuals making arbitrary sets of commitments. But as H. Richard Niebuhr suggests, the self is social; the fundamental form of the social self is the face-to-face community where unlimited commitments are the rule and in which every facet of the self is shaped by membership in the interpersonal group. Persons discover who they are in relationship with others in love, work, and learning. Therefore, if persons live in stories and use master images that do not include communal figures such as covenant, then it is difficult for them to imagine the truth that human action goes on in a storied web of relationships.[87]

Whether the woman-as-person figure has the resources to combat self-deception depends, then, upon the context in which it is set. If woman-as-person is seen from the angle of vision of the contemporary story of well-being, then its resources to combat self-deception are as problematic as the resources of the story of well-being itself.

But if, the figure of woman-as-person is set in the covenant language of biblical story, it draws resources from that story to combat the inveterate human tendency to self-deception. The context of the image is thus the crucial issue. The wide acceptance in American culture of the image of woman-as-person in the context of covenant would spell the end of woman-as-outsider. Women, like men, would then share equally in the task of drawing upon the resources in American culture to know themselves and guide their action. But today American culture remains largely patriarchal. Therefore, woman is still outsider, and still at risk in American society.

7

Conclusion

As I noted in the introduction, because I was interested in social ethics the first question that I put to my congregation in the sixties was this: "In light of the biblical narrative, how ought we to guide our action?" But as I discovered that we saw the central issues of contemporary life so differently, I began to raise a prior set of questions. "How do we understand ourselves and the world in which we live? How have we become the persons we are? Why do we see the world in the way we see it?" This way of formulating the central issue in social ethics had been strongly influenced by H. Richard Niebuhr.

For Niebuhr, when we take up the task of ethics, we seek both to know ourselves and to guide our action. Thereby we decide, choose, commit ourselves, and otherwise bear the burden of our necessary human freedom. The knowledge of self, Niebuhr argues, depends upon the recognition that we are social, historical, dependent selves, who seek the integrity of self amidst multiple cultural demands. In order to respond in a fitting way to what is going on in our world, we must first understand the communities and culture in which we dwell.[1]

From such a perspective, the adequacy of our ethics depends upon the adequacy of the images that we think with about self and world. Three convictions emerge from this study: (1) The cultural narratives are inherently conservative, (2) narrative is the form of rationality especially appropriate for ethics, and (3) we not only can, but must make judgments that one story is more adequate than another.

First, cultural narratives are inherently conservative. Even though the minorities draw upon rich cultural resources to reorder the cultural vision of the majority, we continue to live in a world shaped by inadequate narratives. It is very difficult to break out of the old way of envisioning the world.

The cultural narratives are not easily refashioned because our experience is always a learning or an appropriation before it is a creating. We are shaped by our culture. We learn to sing and then discover that the music we sing is in a scale. We learn a language, and then find that we both think and speak within the confines of a particular grammar. We learn stories, and then notice that we interpret life itself from within the sense of the whole that is given to us in the stories. In a larger sense, what we discover, learn, and notice is that the cultural narratives provide a world for us to inhabit. This world encompasses our individual biographies, which unfold as events within that world. Our own lives appear meaningful to us only as they are located within the socially constructed world of the cultural narratives. They provide the context in which our actions have meaning.

In turn, in our own time, we participate in those actions that produce culture. Together we write music, invent stories, shape tools, and devise institutions. It is these ongoing human actions that create the world in which we dwell. Our actions are usually in accord with the world in which we originally awakened. We draw that world into ourselves, identify with it, and take it up as our own personal perspective. Thus as we become the persons who represent and express the culture, we carry on the cultural narratives we have been taught. Conserving the vision we learned, we now teach the next generation the language in which it will think. We create the families, celebrate the religion, establish the schools, take up the work, and tell the life stories that provide the images of self and world for our children.[2]

The life stories that we tell allow others to grasp the connection between our understanding of our selves—that is, our character—and the cultural narratives in which we live. Life stories are accounts of our speech and action, intentions, and sufferings, which take place within a particular world. Our character emerges as we develop certain patterns in our actions and in our responses to sufferings. Sufferings often come upon us because of the actions of others, but we also suffer from acts of nature and the frailty of our bodies. It is in discerning the patterns of action and response that we and others come to know who we are. When we become characters whose actions and responses to sufferings can be followed within the logic of our life story, we also begin to see the structure or character of the world we have constructed. So as Benjamin Franklin writes his *Autobiography,* he affirms that the world is truly a world of progress. Life stories reveal this sense of the whole.[3]

Even though cultural narratives are conservative and patterns emerge within our life stories, we are all aware of how full of surprises life is. We recognize that our actions take place in a world of conflict with others who also have the ability to initiate new courses of events. Although we come to know who we or others are in a story and what sort of world the story has fashioned, we are not able to predict the actions of the characters (including ourselves!) nor the outcome of their intentions or actions. The logic of a story enables us, however, to pursue the characters and their actions through unexpected twists and turns. We can see that they are leading us to a conclusion, even though a particular conclusion cannot be predicted and is not required by their action. Thus a story binds together even surprising events and unexpected actions of the characters into an intelligible pattern.

Now we can account for our second conviction, that narratives are the form of rationality especially appropriate for ethics. Since human action includes pattern and structure and the surprising and the unexpected, narratives are required in order to adequately conserve and reflect upon that action with a logic that is appropriate to it. We inquire into our experience with the figure of story, and with the same figure we grope toward the discovery of who we are and the character of the world in which we live. Only narratives take account of this logic of human action—a logic that includes both the expected and the unexpected. Therefore, as Hauerwas remarks, narratives have the capacity to order life with an appropriate logic, to unfold or develop character, and to offer insight into the human condition. For these reasons, narrative is the form of rationality especially appropriate for ethics.[4]

We now need to reflect on the third conviction that emerges from our study: We not only can, but must make judgments that one story is more adequate than another. Because we live in a culture that has competing cultural narratives, life stories or autobiographies that deal with the movement from story to story include a recounting of how one comes to judge certain stories as better than others. Such a recounting demonstrates that we believe that a story helps us develop certain skills of perception and understanding, which relate us to the world and form our intentions to modify it. The movement from story to story always involves an assent of faith—a conviction that one story is more adequate than another in enabling one to recognize truth and to conform one's character to that truth.[5]

This conviction arises because there is a connection between cultural narratives, the metaphors that emerge from them, and truth. Each cultural narrative has a master image or central metaphor. Although there are many images in each narrative, the master image provides a distillation of the story; it enables us to grasp concretely and practically what the story means. The master image serves as a metaphor with which to think about self and world. Because a cultural narrative is such an extended story, we use the master image or central metaphor to help us evaluate the adequacy of the narrative.[6]

The task of evaluating master images or metaphors is common to many disciplines. Science, poetry, art, history, religion, philosophy, and politics all have a tradition and a method by which they seek to understand the universe and human beings. Students of metaphor such as Sallie McFague, Elizabeth Sewell, and Michael Polanyi agree that good metaphors are heuristic: that is, they enable us to go on asking questions, to think with the freshness that precedes discovery, and to hope we are about to break out of our old inadequate way of interpreting life into a new vision of reality.[7]

Elizabeth Sewell has given an example of a metaphor that was exact, that fit a particular experience, but was unsatisfactory because it was not heuristic. As she was trying to find a metaphor for a poem, she hit upon one: The foliage of the autumn trees has precisely the color range of the blossoms on the springtime azaleas. She was delighted with the exactitude, yet she was disappointed later. The metaphor, though exact, did not enable her to go on asking, thinking, and hoping. All she could do with the metaphor was to note its application to a particular experience, and then leave it there.[8]

Sewell's distinction between an exact metaphor and a heuristic one is useful in reflecting on the cultural narratives. As we think about self and world with the story of success, we can see that its master image is an exact metaphor for some experiences. The claim that hard work is the key to success is true for most of us in some aspects of our lives, such as education, athletics, or sales. But the metaphor does not enable us to inquire about the gifts given us, such as intelligence, coordination, or personal attractiveness. It does not encourage us to go on thinking with the freshness that precedes discovery about the desperate poverty that abounds in our country and in the third world. It does not awaken in us the hope and desire to break out of our old self-deceptive framework, which congratulates the successful for their hard work and blames the poor for their poverty.

Likewise, the story of well-being provides an exact metaphor for some of life's experiences. The master image of the story of well-being is that the good life consists of using therapeutic resources to nurture one's sense of well-being. It is true for most of us that in personal relationships, whether on the job or among family and friends, life is better if the relationships display the therapeutic values of communication, empathy, and authenticity. But the metaphor does not enable us to inquire into the meaning of suffering or to go on thinking in a fresh way about how rich and poor, black and white, men and women, Americans and Nicaraguans are bound together in a common destiny. Therefore the story of well-being does not awaken in us the hope and desire to break out of the self-deception of radical individualism.

The story of the mission of America is also, in its own way, an exact metaphor for the relationship between America and the world. America has been an example of freedom to others. Peoples from around the world have poured into this land in order to share the American experience. America has defended the freedom of others. From the Normandy beaches to the small town of Badonviller, near the Rhine, there are monuments that express appreciation for Americans who died that France might be free. But the master image that America is to defend freedom around the world does not enable us to inquire into why we include cruel oppressive regimes in the "free world" that we defend; the claim that we are an example to the world does not encourage us to think in a fresh way about how American economic interests have reaped enormous profits in third-world countries; the claim that America has a mission to the world has not awakened in us the hope and desire to break out of the self-deceptive framework that has carried us into war after war.

In contrast, Polanyi gives us an example of a metaphor that is heuristic. His example is based on his argument that human beings construct frameworks, such as cultural narratives or scientific theories, with which to interpret experience. When we discover a new way of interpreting reality, we break out of the old framework in an intense moment of heuristic vision. Copernicus's discovery that the universe is heliocentric is an example of a breaking out of the old geocentric framework with a heuristic metaphor. The new metaphor enables us to keep on discovering more and more of the truth about what is going on in our universe.[9]

As we have seen, the general trend for human beings is to settle down in a familiar interpretative framework and allow that framework to handle experience. The geocentric metaphor is an excellent example of how an inadequate framework can survive across the centuries. Cultural narratives also survive across the centuries as inadequate frameworks.

However, according to Polanyi, the biblical story differs from any other framework of inherent excellence in that the story itself works against those who would settle down in the story and allow it to handle experience. The storying of experience in terms of covenant gift and the subsequent requirement that the character of the faithful person be conformed to the character of the Covenant Giver induces a state of tension. As persons dwell in this story, they are continually confronted with their inability to love God with all their heart, soul, mind, and strength and to love their neighbors as themselves. Such is the human condition. If persons were to claim they had reached the level of perfection demanded, they would be thrown back into spiritual emptiness and called to account by the biblical stories of self-deception.

Perhaps the best-known story that displays the emptiness of a person who claims to have fully met the demands of the covenant is the story of the Pharisee and the tax collector at prayer in the temple. The Pharisee thanks God that he is so righteous. The tax collector prays, "God, be merciful to me a sinner." Jesus concludes the story by declaring that the tax collector went home at rights with God, while the Pharisee did not. Thus the character of biblical story works against the desire to settle down and be comfortable in it.

Polanyi concludes that those who dwell in the biblical framework continually attempt to break out of this human condition of self-centeredness, even while humbly acknowledging its inescapability. The more persons seek to dwell in the biblical story, the more they seek to break out of the human condition. Dwelling in the biblical story, therefore, resembles the heuristic upsurge that strives to break through accepted frameworks of thought. Biblical story, Polanyi says, sustains "an eternal, never to be consummated hunch: a heuristic vision which is accepted for the sake of its unresolvable tension."[10]

Translated into biblical terms, this means that God always loves us in grace-full ways. God is always beginning over again with us, giving us, though we do not deserve it, the gift of the covenant, the gift of the kingdom. And with the new beginning, with the gift, comes the gift of the Spirit, that we might conform our lives, as did Jesus, to the character of the Giver. Thus, over and over again we find ourselves in a situation in which we are enabled to go on asking questions about the character of a true life, to think with the freshness that precedes discovery about how the life of Jesus displays that truth, and to hope that we are about to break out of our old inadequate way of interpreting life into a new vision of the way God rules the world.

Polanyi's example is grounded in his conviction that truth itself is a personal affirmation. To say "truth is a personal affirmation" is to use a human metaphor, and to awaken in the hearer the possibility of understanding that the logic of truth, like the logic of narrative, is personal. Since to speak of "truth" is to speak of a universal reality, to also include the personal in the definition of truth is a perspective that is quite different from a framework that divides the world between the objective and subjective.

Polanyi's use of a personal metaphor in understanding truth enables us to see that the search for truth is not a search for an objective reality, but an ongoing task within the context of community and culture. Therefore, when we, in ethics or in science, intend to discover and assert a universal truth, we do so from within a particular community's framework of interpretation. When we break out of the old framework, discovery makes us into persons who see and think differently. We see the world anew.[11]

The experience of discovery demonstrates that we are

able to move from one interpretative framework to another. The move is made within the context of commitment: As I interpret the meaning of my actions and sufferings, as I make explicit the story that serves as a framework for that interpretation, I intend by means of this action to assert a universal truth: namely, that this story is the true story with which to understand the human condition. Such an assertion claims to establish contact with reality beyond the clues on which it relies and commits me to a vision of reality.

My personal participation in making such an affirmation is compensated for by my claim that I am submitting to the universal status of the hidden reality that I am asserting. Of course, I may be mistaken. Perhaps I cannot make a responsible judgment with universal intent when my whole being has been so shaped by the stories of the culture in which I awakened. But such are the limits of the human condition. To inquire into how I might think if I were not born into this culture or this body is as meaningless as to inquire into what human life might be like if it had no limits. I must accept the limits as the gift and challenge of being human, and evaluate the cultural narratives in which I have come to know myself and to guide my action.[12]

As we undertake that evaluation, the question that we must ask of each cultural narrative is whether the narrative provides the resources to cope with self-deception. Stephen Crites quite rightly points out that if we imagine that there is a "solution" to this "problem" we have not understood that "self-deception is a permanent possibility implicit in the very dynamics of experience . . . it is a predicament that we must learn to live with."[13] To be is to be self-deceived.

Therefore, we evaluate the adequacy of a cultural narrative by taking up the argument that "a good metaphor is a heuristic metaphor" and applying that insight to the issue of self-deception. We notice that some cultural stories provide more adequate accounts of how persons take up cover stories, and that, with the aid of those in their communities who take up the vocation of truth telling, persons discover ways to return to the real story. Such stories enable us to gain the experience and the skill required to recognize our own self-deception, and to be more faithful to the truth more of the time. The more adequately the cultural story deals with self-deception, the more heuristic are its master images for ethics.

The suggestions for coping with self-deception that emerge from this study are not new to American culture. They have been made in every generation since Ann Hutchinson. First, we need to renew our attempts to learn from that cultural narrative that deals again and again with self-deception, the biblical story. Second, we need to renew our willingness to listen seriously to the outsiders, whose lives and words reveal the many ways we bend our vision of the good to our own self-interest. With such resources we can take up anew the art of ethics—the knowing of ourselves and the guiding of our action.

Notes

Chapter 1: Introduction

1. I am using "American" in the way it is commonly used in texts in American history, American studies, and the history of religion in America. Such usage confines "American" primarily to the United States of America, with only occasional reference to Mexico and Canada. That such a tradition exists with all its attendant problems displays the staying power of the "mission of America." For a different way of imagining the diversity of the sixties, see my earlier study, *The Radical Movement of the 1960s* (when not given here, full facts of publication appear in the Bibliography).

2. Marcus G. Raskin and Bernard B. Fall, eds., *The Viet-Nam Reader.*

3. Betty Friedan, *The Feminine Mystique;* see also the study of "his marriage" and "her marriage" by Jessie Bernard, *The Future of Marriage* (New York: Bantam Books, 1972).

4. H. Richard Niebuhr, *The Responsible Self,* has strongly influenced my understanding of ethics. See also Stanley Hauerwas, *A Community of Character,* especially ch. 5, "The Church in a Divided World," pp. 89–110.

5. Clifford Geertz, *The Interpretation of Cultures,* pp. 89, 52.

6. Ibid.; Stephen Crites, "The Narrative Quality of Experience," pp. 294–297.

7. Philip Rieff, *The Triumph of the Therapeutic,* p. 4.

8. Robert Bellah et al., *Habits of the Heart;* Geertz, *Cultures.*

9. There is a considerable literature that develops each of these perspectives, although in differing ways. Rieff, *Triumph,* develops four character ideals that arise out of the narrative of each of four periods in Western civilization; Bellah, *Habits,* takes up Rieff's

typology but attempts to make a case for a contemporary "civic republicanism"; I am convinced that civic responsibility is a calling that is imagined as part of the larger whole of the biblical, Enlightenment, or mission narratives. Ralph Henry Gabriel, *The Course of American Democratic Thought,* among others, supports this point of view.

Gabriel, Russel B. Nye in *This Almost Chosen People,* and many others make the case for the mission of America. Henry F. May, *The Enlightenment in America* and *Ideas, Faiths and Feelings,* and Henry Steele Commager, *Jefferson, Nationalism, and the Enlightenment,* discuss the Enlightenment in American culture. Max Weber, *The Protestant Ethic and the Spirit of Capitalism;* Irvin G. Wyllie, *The Self-made Man in America;* Brian M. Barbour, ed., *Benjamin Franklin: A Collection of Critical Essays;* and Charles L. Sanford, *Benjamin Franklin and the American Character,* all take up the Enlightenment and the story of success.

The blending of the Enlightenment and biblical stories in a "civil religion" is addressed by Martin E. Marty, *Pilgrims in Their Own Land,* pp. 154–166; Winthrop S. Hudson, *Religion in America* (New York: Macmillan Co., 1987), pp. 107–126; Sidney Mead, *The Nation with the Soul of a Church* and *The Lively Experiment;* Robert Bellah, *Beyond Belief,* pp. 168–189, and *The Broken Covenant;* Conrad Cherry, *God's New Israel;* Russell E. Richey and Donald G. Jones, *American Civil Religion.*

Many authors discuss the twentieth century as an age of well-being, including Rieff, *Triumph;* Bellah, *Habits;* Alasdair MacIntyre, *After Virtue;* T. J. Jackson Lears, *No Place of Grace;* Richard Wightman Fox and T. J. Jackson Lears, eds., *The Culture of Consumption;* Warren Susman, *Culture as History;* Daniel Yankelovich, *New Rules.*

10. Peter L. Berger, *The Sacred Canopy.*

11. Ibid., pp. 29–51.

12. W. E. B. Du Bois, *The Souls of Black Folk.*

13. Stephen Crites, "The Aesthetics of Self-Deception," pp. 107ff; M. Bruce Haddox, "Self, Society and Stories: Reflections on Thinking."

14. Crites, "Aesthetics."

15. Reinhold Niebuhr discusses the theme of self-deception in relation to national communities in a somewhat different way in *Moral Man and Immoral Society* and *The Irony of American History.*

Chapter 2: The Biblical Story

1. Perry Miller, *Errand Into the Wilderness,* pp. 48–98.
2. John Winthrop, "A Model of Christian Charity," in Perry Miller, ed., *The American Puritans,* p. 83.
3. Ibid., p. 84.
4. William G. McLoughlin, *Revivals, Awakenings, and Reform* (Chicago: University of Chicago Press, 1978), pp. 1–140.
5. Walter Brueggemann, *The Land,* pp. 15–150. Note especially Brueggemann's discussion of the land as gift, temptation, task, and threat in ch. 4, "Reflections at the Boundary."
6. Bernard Anderson, *Understanding the Old Testament,* 4th ed. (Englewood Cliffs, N.J.: Prentice-Hall, 1986), pp. 376–386.
7. Charles H. Talbert, *Reading Luke.*
8. John Howard Yoder, *The Politics of Jesus.*
9. John Dominic Crossan, *In Parables,* p. 64.
10. Ibid., pp. 119–120.

Chapter 3: The Gospel of Success in America

1. Henry F. May, *The Enlightenment in America,* p. xvi, and *Ideas, Faiths and Feelings,* p. 126.
2. Henry Steele Commager, *Jefferson, Nationalism, and the Enlightenment,* p. 4.
3. Martin E. Marty, *Pilgrims in Their Own Land,* pp. 154–166; Winthrop S. Hudson, *Religion in America* (New York: Macmillan Co., 1987), pp. 107–126; Sidney Mead, *The Nation with the Soul of a Church* and *The Lively Experiment;* Robert N. Bellah, *Beyond Belief,* pp. 168–189, and *The Broken Covenant;* Conrad Cherry, *God's New Israel;* and Russell E. Richey and Donald G. Jones, *American Civil Religion.*
4. Benjamin Franklin, *The Autobiography of Benjamin Franklin,* p. 90.
5. Marty, *Pilgrims,* p. 160.
6. Bellah, *Belief,* p. 174.
7. May, *Enlightenment,* p. xvii.
8. Ralph Henry Gabriel, *The Course of American Democratic Thought,* pp. 12–25.
9. Ibid., p. 20.
10. Max Weber, *The Protestant Ethic and the Spirit of Capitalism,* pp. 48–49.
11. Irvin G. Wyllie, *The Self-made Man in America,* p. 15.

12. John William Ward, "Benjamin Franklin: The Making of an American Character," in Brian M. Barbour, ed., *Benjamin Franklin: A Collection of Critical Essays,* pp. 50–62.

13. Charles L. Sanford, *Benjamin Franklin and the American Character,* p. 72; David Levin, "The Autobiography of Benjamin Franklin," in Barbour, ed., *Franklin,* pp. 75–92.

14. Carl Van Doren, *Benjamin Franklin,* p. 69; Michael T. Gilmore, "Franklin and the Shaping of American Theology," in Barbour, ed., *Franklin,* pp. 105–124.

15. Franklin, *Autobiography,* p. 98.

16. Bellah, *Habits,* pp. 40–41; Alice Tyler, *Freedom's Ferment.*

17. Weber, *Ethic,* p. 108.

18. Cotton Mather, *Bonifacius: An Essay to Do Good.*

19. Weber, *Ethic,* p. 108.

20. Bellah, *Broken Covenant,* pp. 68–76.

21. William Holmes McGuffey, *McGuffey's Fifth Eclectic Reader,* p. 231.

22. Bellah, *Habits,* pp. 42–44; Wyllie, *Self-made Man,* p. 4.

23. Cherry, *Israel,* pp. 211–271; Mead, *Experiment,* pp. 156–187.

24. Andrew Carnegie, "Wealth," pp. 653–664.

25. Ibid., p. 666.

26. Ibid., p. 671.

27. Donald Fleming, "Social Darwinism," in *Paths of American Thought,* by Arthur M. Schlesinger, Jr., and Morton M. White, pp. 124–125; Andrew Carnegie, *Autobiography;* Charles Darwin, *The Descent of Man* (New York: Collier Books, 1901) and *On the Origin of Species* (New York: Collier Books, 1901).

28. Cherry, *Israel,* p. 246–250.

29. Carnegie, *Autobiography,* p. 327.

30. Ibid.

31. Joseph F. Wall, *Andrew Carnegie,* p. 138.

32. Ibid., pp. 141–142.

Chapter 4: The Story of Well-being

1. T. J. Jackson Lears, *No Place of Grace,* pp. 55–56; Richard Wightman Fox and T. J. Jackson Lears, eds., *The Culture of Consumption,* pp. 3–38.

2. Henry David Thoreau, *Walden* (Garden City, N.Y.: Doubleday & Co., Anchor Books, 1973), p. 134.

3. Alan Trachtenberg, *The Incorporation of America,* pp. 3, 4.

4. Alasdair MacIntyre, *After Virtue*, pp. 28–30.

5. Peter Homans refers to this development as the rise of the culture of narcissism. See Homans, *Jung in Context*, pp. 193–196; Lears, *Grace*, p. 34; Warren Susman, *Culture as History*, p. 218.

6. Lears, *Grace*, p. 42.

7. Susman, *History*, pp. 273–277; Robert N. Bellah, *Habits of the Heart*, pp. 113–141.

8. James Hillman, "The Fiction of Case History: A Round," in James Wiggins, ed., *Religion as Story*, pp. 123–173.

9. Philip Rieff, *The Triumph of the Therapeutic*, pp. 29–107.

10. Ibid., pp. 29–47.

11. Ibid., pp. 79–107.

12. Ibid., pp. 48–107; Hillman, "Fiction," pp. 130–132.

13. Rieff, *Triumph*, pp. 108–140.

14. Bellah, *Habits*, pp. 208–211; Richard Hofstadter, *The Progressive Movement*, pp. 1–16; Susman, *History*, p. 92.

15. Richard Weiss, *The American Myth of Success*, p. 222.

16. Bellah, *Habits*, p. 122.

17. Ibid., pp. 122–123.

18. Fox and Lears, *Consumption*, pp. 3, 4.

19. Ibid., pp. 17–30.

20. Ibid., p. ix.

21. Rieff, *Triumph*, p. 13.

22. Fox and Lears, *Consumption*, pp. 28–29.

23. Ibid., pp. 30–38.

24. Ibid., pp. 33, 34.

25. Susman, *History*, p. 128.

26. Ibid.

27. Harry Emerson Fosdick, *Adventurous Religion*, pp. 18, 264; cf. Fox and Lears, *Consumption*, p. 14.

28. Fosdick, *Religion*, p. 28.

29. Ibid.

30. Donald Meyer, *The Positive Thinkers*, pp. 211–219.

31. Norman Vincent Peale, *The Power of Positive Thinking*, p. x.

32. Ibid., pp. 93–94.

33. Richard Weiss, *The American Myth of Success*, p. 229.

34. Robert H. Schuller, *Tough Times Never Last, but Tough People Do!*, p. 1.

35. Ibid., pp. 57–71.

36. Robert H. Schuller, *Self-Esteem*, p. 19.

37. Ibid., pp. 48–51.

38. Christopher Lasch, *The Culture of Narcissism*, p. 330.

39. Ibid., p. 340.

40. Nena and George O'Neill, *Open Marriage,* pp. 38–41.

41. Ibid., pp. 148, 224–235.

42. Stanley Hauerwas, *A Community of Character,* pp. 180–182.

43. Frank Kermode, *The Sense of an Ending;* Dale Cannon, "Ruminations on the Claim of Inerrability"; Albert Camus, *The Plague* (New York: Vintage Books, 1972); Will Herberg, *Protestant, Catholic, Jew,* pp. 263–267.

44. Arthur Miller, *Death of a Salesman,* p. 81.

45. Lasch, *Narcissism,* p. 391.

46. Bellah, *Habits,* pp. 83–84, 295.

Chapter 5: The Mission of America

1. John F. Kennedy, "Inaugural Address," pp. 5, 6.

2. Ibid.

3. See "Cultural Narratives" in chapter 1. Also see Clifford Geertz, *The Interpretation of Cultures,* p. 52; Peter L. Berger, *The Sacred Canopy,* pp. 29–51.

4. Russel B. Nye, *This Almost Chosen People,* p. 168.

5. Ralph Henry Gabriel, *The Course of American Democratic Thought,* p. 25.

6. J. F. Maclear, "The Republic and the Millennium," in E. A. Smith, ed., *The Religion of the Republic,* pp. 183–216.

7. Ibid., pp. 190–216.

8. Jonathan Edwards, "The Latter-Day Glory Is Probably to Begin in America," in Conrad Cherry, *God's New Israel,* pp. 55–60.

9. Sidney Mead, *The Lively Experiment,* pp. 134–155.

10. Winthrop S. Hudson, *Religion in America* (New York: Macmillan Co., 1987), pp. 60–194; Alice Tyler, *Freedom's Ferment.*

11. Henry Steele Commager, *Jefferson, Nationalism, and the Enlightenment,* pp. 77–121.

12. Robert Bellah, *Habits of the Heart,* pp. 31, 32.

13. Ibid., p. 74.

14. William G. McLoughlin, *Revivals, Awakening, and Reform,* p. 105.

15. Herman Melville, *White Jacket,* quoted in Ernest L. Tuveson, *Redeemer Nation,* p. 157.

16. Ronald A. Wells, ed., *The Wars of America,* p. 1.

17. Ronald Steel, *Pax Americana,* p. xi.

18. Abraham Lincoln, "The Second Inaugural Address," in *The Annals of America,* vol. 9 (Chicago: Encyclopaedia Britannica, 1968), p. 556.

19. Reinhold Niebuhr, *Moral Man and Immoral Society,* pp. 95–97.

20. National Conference of Catholic Bishops, *The Challenge of Peace,* pp. 1–25.

21. Martin Luther King, Jr., *Stride Toward Freedom;* William D. Miller, *Dorothy Day: A Biography.*

22. Catholic Bishops, *Peace,* pp. 25–37.

23. Roland H. Bainton, *Christian Attitudes Toward War and Peace;* Edward LeRoy Long, *War and Conscience in America.*

24. Ronald A. Wells, ed., *The Wars of America,* pp. 45–66; Frederick Merk, *Manifest Destiny and Mission in American History.*

25. Merk, *Manifest,* pp. 81–82.

26. Wells, *Wars,* p. 58.

27. Josiah Royce, *California, a Study in American Character* (Boston: Houghton Mifflin Co., 1886), p. 151, quoted in Wells, *Wars,* pp. 64–65.

28. Ibid., p. 64.

29. Augustus Cerillo, Jr., "The Spanish-American War," in Wells, *Wars,* pp. 91–126.

30. Albert J. Beveridge, "The Taste of Empire," in the *Annals of America,* vol. 12, p. 202.

31. Josiah Strong, *Our Country,* pp. 71–76.

32. Cerillo, "Spanish-American," p. 121.

33. Niebuhr, *Moral Man,* p. 99.

34. Nye, *Chosen People,* p. 200.

35. Ibid.

36. Ibid., p. 201.

37. Franklin D. Roosevelt, "Annual Message to Congress," in Conrad Cherry, *God's New Israel,* pp. 297–298.

38. Roger G. Betsworth, *The Radical Movement of the 1960s,* pp. 122–131.

39. Arthur M. Schlesinger, Jr., *A Thousand Days: John F. Kennedy in the White House,* p. 769.

40. Mike Gravel, ed., *The Pentagon Papers: The Defense Department History of United States Decisionmaking on Vietnam,* vol. 1, pp. 472–476.

41. Ibid., vol. 2, p. 22.

42. Ibid., vol. 2, pp. 17–127.

43. Lyndon B. Johnson, *The Vantage Point,* pp. 43ff.

44. Ibid., p. 344.

45. C. L. Cooper, *The Lost Crusade: America in Vietnam,* p. 452.

46. Senator J. W. Fulbright, *The Arrogance of Power,* pp. 106, 107, 258.

47. Eugene J. McCarthy, *The Year of the People;* Jack Newfield, *Robert Kennedy: A Memoir,* pp. 140–141; Arthur M. Schlesinger, Jr., *Robert Kennedy and His Times,* vol. 2, pp. 806–808.

48. Robert Bolt, "American Involvement in World War I," in Wells, *Wars,* p. 138.

49. Catholic Bishops, *Peace,* p. 16.

50. Ibid., pp. 16, 17.

51. Ibid., pp. 20–37. See also Stanley Hauerwas, *Against the Nations* (Minneapolis: Winston Press, 1985), pp. 169–198.

52. Catholic Bishops, *Peace,* p. 5.

53. The United Methodist Council of Bishops, *In Defense of Creation: The Nuclear Crisis and a Just Peace,* p. 36.

54. Ibid., pp. 52, 53.

55. Ibid., p. 63; Catholic Bishops, *Peace,* p. 80.

56. Ibid., p. 98.

57. Niebuhr, *Moral Man,* pp. 91, 92.

Chapter 6: The Outsiders

1. Peter L. Berger, *The Sacred Canopy,* pp. 3–51.

2. Ibid., pp. 95–101.

3. Vincent Harding, *There Is a River.*

4. Vincent Harding, "Out of the Cauldron of Struggle," p. 340.

5. George D. Kelsey, *Racism and the Christian Understanding of Man,* pp. 23–25.

6. Peter J. Paris, *The Social Teaching of the Black Churches,* pp. 27–29.

7. W. E. B. Du Bois, *The Souls of Black Folk,* pp. 16, 17.

8. Paris, *Social Teaching,* p. 29.

9. Albert C. Outler, ed., *John Wesley* (New York: Oxford University Press, 1964), p. 86.

10. Harding, *River;* Gayraud S. Wilmore, *Black Religion and Black Radicalism.*

11. Harding, *River,* pp. 75–100; Stephen B. Oates, *The Fires of Jubilee* (New York: Mentor Books, 1975); Wilmore, *Black Radicalism,* pp. 62–72.

12. Harding, *River*, p. 89.

13. Ibid., pp. 86, 87.

14. Ibid., pp. 88, 89.

15. Albert J. Raboteau, "Martin Luther King, Jr., and the Tradition of Black Religious Protest," paper delivered at the Project on Religion and the Nation, Indiana University—Purdue University at Indianapolis, Indianapolis, September 1985, p. 5.

16. Ibid., pp. 103–188.

17. Wilmore, *Black Radicalism*, pp. 122–138.

18. Harding, "Cauldron," pp. 344–345; Albert J. Raboteau, "Ethiopia Shall Soon Stretch Forth Her Hands: Black Destiny in Nineteenth Century America," the University Lecture in Religion, Arizona State University, January 27, 1983.

19. Raboteau, "Black Destiny," pp. 1, 2.

20. Ibid., p. 3.

21. Harding, *River*, p. 50.

22. Paris, *Social Teaching*.

23. William Holmes McGuffey, *McGuffey's Fifth Eclectic Reader*, p. 231; Paris, *Social Teaching*, pp. 1–56; August Meier et al., eds., *Black Protest Thought in the Twentieth Century*, 2nd ed. (Indianapolis: Bobbs-Merrill Co., 1965), pp. xix–xxix, 3–17.

24. Raboteau, "King," p. 12.

25. Wilmore, *Black Radicalism*, pp. 135–166.

26. Marcus Garvey, quoted in Meier et al., eds., *Thought*, p. 102.

27. Marcus Garvey, quoted in Amy Jacques-Garvey, ed., *Philosophy and Opinions of Marcus Garvey*, p. 3.

28. Randall K. Burkett, *Garveyism as a Religious Movement;* Raboteau, "King," pp. 14, 15.

29. Wilmore, *Black Radicalism*, pp. 169–170.

30. Malcolm X, *The Autobiography of Malcolm X*, p. 180.

31. Ibid., p. 266.

32. Ibid., p. 272.

33. Ibid., p. 374.

34. Harding, "Cauldron," p. 347.

35. Martin Luther King, Jr., *Stride Toward Freedom*, p. 101.

36. Ibid., pp. 100–107.

37. Martin Luther King, Jr., "Letter from Birmingham Jail," in Milton C. Sernett, *Afro-American Religious History: A Documentary Witness* (Durham: Duke University Press, 1985), pp. 430–445.

38. King, *Stride*, p. 359.

39. King, "Letter," p. 443.

40. Stephen B. Oates, *Let the Trumpet Sound: The Life of Martin Luther King, Jr.*, p. 290.

41. Ibid., p. 436.

42. Ibid., p. 434.

43. Ibid., p. 436.

44. Martin Luther King, Jr., "I Have a Dream," in Meier et al., eds., *Thought,* p. 349.

45. Harding, "Cauldron," p. 351.

46. James H. Cone, *God of the Oppressed;* James H. Cone, ed., *Speaking the Truth: Ecumenism, Liberation, and Black Theology* (Grand Rapids: Wm. B. Eerdmans Publishing Co., 1986).

47. Rosemary Radford Ruether, *New Woman—New Earth: Sexist Ideologies and Human Liberation,* pp. 3–31; cf. Introduction, pp. 28–29.

48. Berger, *Canopy,* pp. 3–51.

49. Ibid., pp. 53–101; Martha Tomhave Blauvelt, "Women and Revivalism," in Rosemary Radford Ruether and Rosemary Skinner Keller, eds., *Women and Religion in America,* vol. 1, pp. 9, 10.

50. Rosemary Skinner Keller, "New England Women: Ideology and Experience in First-Generation Puritanism (1630–1650)," in Ruether and Keller, eds., *Women and Religion in America,* vol. 2, pp. 132–192; Mary P. Ryan, *Womanhood in America,* p. 4.

51. Ryan, *Womanhood,* pp. 12–40; Barbara J. MacHaffie, *Her Story,* pp. 77–80.

52. Keller, "New England Women," pp. 139–140.

53. Selma R. Williams, *Divine Rebel: The Life of Anne Marbury Hutchinson;* Emery Battis, *Saints and Sectaries: Anne Hutchinson and the Antinomian Controversy,* p. 92; Janet Wilson James, ed., *Women in American Religion,* pp. 30–31.

54. Margaret Hope Bacon, *Mothers of Feminism: The Story of Quaker Women in America,* pp. 5–23.

55. Elisabeth Griffith, *In Her Own Right: The Life of Elizabeth Cady Stanton;* Elisabeth Schüssler Fiorenza, *In Memory of Her,* pp. 7–13; MacHaffie, *Her Story,* pp. 108–110.

56. Fiorenza, *Her.*

57. Beverly Wildung Harrison, *Making the Connections,* pp. 42–54.

58. Eleanor Flexner, *Century of Struggle,* pp. 148–149.

59. Blauvelt, "Women and Revivalism," pp. 1–9.

60. Gerda Lerner, *The Grimké Sisters from South Carolina.*

61. Ibid., p. 7.

62. Flexner, *Century*, pp. 142–155.

63. Griffith, *In Her Own Right*, pp. 102–104.

64. Ryan, *Womanhood*, pp. 118–150.

65. Anzia Yezierska, *Bread Givers*, p. xiii.

66. Ibid., p. 16.

67. Ibid., p. 206.

68. Ibid., p. 297.

69. Allen F. Davis, *American Heroine*, p. 20.

70. Jane Addams, *Twenty Years at Hull-House*, p. xiv.

71. Ryan, *Womanhood*, pp. 149–150.

72. Jessie Bernard, *The Future of Marriage* (New York: Bantam Books, 1972), p. 51.

73. Ibid., p. 17.

74. Bellah, *Habits*, p. 96.

75. Ryan, *Womanhood*, p. 160.

76. Friedan, *Mystique*, pp. 27–61.

77. Ibid.

78. Ibid.; Ryan, *Womanhood*, pp. 183–218; Sheila M. Rothman, *Woman's Proper Place*, pp. 224–231.

79. Friedan, *Mystique*, p. 14.

80. Ibid., pp. 69, 71.

81. Ibid., pp. 326, 332–333.

82. Rothman, *Woman's Proper Place*, p. 231.

83. Ibid., p. 259.

84. Ibid., pp. 239–240.

85. Kate Millett, *Sexual Politics;* Gail Sheehy, *Passages* (New York: E. P. Dutton & Co., 1976).

86. Beverly Wildung Harrison, *Our Right to Choose*, pp. 4–10, 229, 255–257.

87. Bellah, *Habits*, pp. 47, 81; H. Richard Niebuhr, *The Responsible Self,* p. 73.

Chapter 7: Conclusion

1. H. Richard Niebuhr, *The Responsible Self.*

2. Peter L. Berger, *The Sacred Canopy*, pp. 29–51.

3. Hannah Arendt, *The Human Condition.*

4. Stanley Hauerwas et al., *Truthfulness and Tragedy*, pp. 15–29, 30, 74–76.

5. Ibid., pp. 34–39.

6. Ibid., pp. 15–39, 82–84.

7. Sallie McFague, *Metaphorical Theology*, pp. 31–42; Michael

Polanyi, *Personal Knowledge;* Elizabeth Sewell, *The Human Metaphor,* pp. 42–75.

8. Sewell, *Metaphor,* p. 59.

9. Polanyi, *Knowledge,* pp. 143, 198.

10. Ibid., pp. 198–199.

11. Ibid. Polanyi develops this theme of congruence in our ways of knowing throughout his study.

12. Polanyi, *Knowledge,* p. 309. According to Polanyi, our limit is not a flaw; it is our means of knowing.

13. Stephen Crites, "The Aesthetics of Self-deception," p. 128.

Bibliography

Addams, Jane. *Twenty Years at Hull-House.* New York: New American Library, 1972.

Alter, Robert. *The Art of Biblical Narrative.* New York: Basic Books, 1981.

Andolsen, Barbara Hilkert, et al., eds. *Women's Consciousness, Women's Conscience.* New York: Harper & Row, 1985.

Arendt, Hannah. *The Human Condition.* Chicago: The University of Chicago Press, 1958.

Arieli, Yehoshua. *Individualism and Nationalism in American Ideology.* Cambridge, Mass.: Harvard University Press, 1964.

Bacon, Margaret Hope. *Mothers of Feminism: The Story of Quaker Women in America.* San Francisco: Harper & Row, 1986.

Bainton, Roland H. *Christian Attitudes Toward War and Peace.* Nashville: Abingdon Press, 1960.

Barbour, Brian M. *Benjamin Franklin: A Collection of Critical Essays.* Englewood Cliffs, N.J.: Prentice-Hall, 1979.

Barton, Bruce. *The Man Nobody Knows.* Indianapolis: Bobbs-Merrill Co., 1924.

Battis, Emery. *Saints and Sectaries: Anne Hutchinson and the Antinomian Controversy.* Chapel Hill, N.C.: University of North Carolina Press, 1962.

Bellah, Robert. *Beyond Belief.* New York: Harper & Row, 1970.

_____. *The Broken Covenant.* New York: Seabury Press, 1975.

_____, et al. *Habits of the Heart.* Berkeley, Calif.: University of California Press, 1986.

Benne, Robert, and Philip Hefner. *Defining America.* Philadelphia: Fortress Press, 1974.

Berger, Peter L. *The Sacred Canopy.* Garden City, N.Y.: Doubleday & Co., Anchor Books, 1969.

Betsworth, Roger G. *The Radical Movement of the 1960s*. Metuchen, N.J.: Scarecrow Press, 1980.

Brueggemann, Walter. *The Land*. Philadelphia: Fortress Press, 1977.

Burkett, Randall K. *Garveyism as a Religious Movement*. Metuchen, N.J.: Scarecrow Press, 1978.

Burns, Edward M. *The American Idea of Mission*. New Brunswick, N.J.: Rutgers University Press, 1957.

Cannon, Dale. "Ruminations on the Claim of Inerrability." *Journal of the American Academy of Religion* 43 (September 4, 1974).

Carnegie, Andrew. *Autobiography*. Boston: Northeastern University Press, 1986.

——. "Wealth." *The North American Review* 391 (June 1889).

Cassirer, Ernst. *The Philosophy of the Enlightenment*. Boston: Beacon Press, 1951.

Cawelti, John G. *Apostles of the Self-made Man*. Chicago: University of Chicago Press, 1965.

Cherry, Conrad. *God's New Israel*. Englewood Cliffs, N.J.: Prentice-Hall, 1971.

Christ, Carol P. *Diving Deep and Surfacing*. Boston: Beacon Press, 1980.

Clebsch, William A. *American Religious Thought*. Chicago: University of Chicago Press, 1973.

Commager, Henry Steele. *The Defeat of America*. New York: Simon & Schuster, 1968.

——. *The Empire of Reason*. Garden City, N.Y.: Doubleday & Co., Anchor Books, 1977.

——. *Jefferson, Nationalism, and the Enlightenment*. New York: George Braziller, 1975.

Cone, James H. *God of the Oppressed*. New York: Seabury Press, 1975.

Conner, Paul W. *Poor Richard's Politics*. New York: Oxford University Press, 1965.

Cooper, C. L. *The Lost Crusade: America in Vietnam*. New York: Dodd, Mead & Co., 1970.

Crites, Stephen. "The Aesthetics of Self-Deception." *Soundings* 62, no. 2 (Summer 1979).

——. "The Narrative Quality of Experience." *Journal of the American Academy of Religion* 39, no. 3 (1971).

Cromwell, Otelia. *Lucretia Mott*. Cambridge, Mass.: Harvard University Press, 1958.

Crossan, Dominic. *The Dark Interval.* Niles, Ill.: Argus Communications, 1975.

_____. *In Parables.* New York: Harper & Row, 1973.

Daly, Mary. *Beyond God the Father.* Boston: Beacon Press, 1973.

_____. *The Church and the Second Sex.* New York: Harper & Row, 1985.

Davis, Allen F. *American Heroine.* Oxford: Oxford University Press, 1973.

Davis, Harry R., and Robert C. Good, eds. *Reinhold Niebuhr on Politics.* New York: Charles Scribner's Sons, 1960.

Day, Dorothy. *The Long Loneliness.* San Francisco: Harper & Row, 1981.

Douglas, Mary, and Steven M. Tipton, eds. *Religion and America.* Boston: Beacon Press, 1982.

Douglass, Ann. *The Feminization of American Culture.* New York: Alfred A. Knopf, 1977.

Du Bois, W. E. B. *The Souls of Black Folk.* Greenwich, Conn.: Fawcett Publications, 1961.

Dulles, Foster R. *America's Rise to World Power.* New York: Harper & Brothers, 1954.

Estess, Ted. "The Inerrable Contraption: Reflections on the Metaphor of Story." *Journal of the American Academy of Religion* 42 (September 1974).

Evans, Sara. *Personal Politics.* New York: Alfred A. Knopf, 1979.

Fingarette, Herbert. *Self-Deception.* London: Routledge & Kegan Paul, 1969.

Fiorenza, Elisabeth Schüssler. *In Memory of Her.* New York: Crossroad Publishing Co., 1987.

Fleming, Donald. "Social Darwinism." In Arthur M. Schlesinger, Jr., and Morton M. White, *Paths of American Thought.* Boston: Houghton Mifflin Co., 1963.

Flexner, Eleanor. *Century of Struggle.* Cambridge, Mass.: Harvard University Press, 1959.

Fosdick, Harry Emerson. *Adventurous Religion.* New York: Harper & Bros., 1926.

Fox, Richard Wightman, and T. J. Jackson Lears, eds. *The Culture of Consumption.* New York: Pantheon Books, 1983.

Franklin, Benjamin. *The Autobiography of Benjamin Franklin.* New York: Airmont Publishing Co., 1965.

Freud, Sigmund. *Civilization and Its Discontents.* New York: W. W. Norton & Co., 1961.

Friedan, Betty. *The Feminine Mystique.* New York: Dell Publishing Co., 1974.

Fulbright, J. W. *The Arrogance of Power.* New York: Random House, 1966.

Funk, Robert W. *Parables and Presence.* Philadelphia: Fortress Press, 1982.

Gabriel, Ralph Henry. *The Course of American Democratic Thought.* 2nd ed. New York: Ronald Press Co., 1956.

Garrow, David J. *Bearing the Cross.* New York: William Morrow & Co., 1986.

Geertz, Clifford. *The Interpretation of Cultures.* New York: Basic Books, 1973.

Goldberg, Michael. *Theology and Narrative.* Nashville: Abingdon Press, 1982.

Gravel, Mike, ed. *The Pentagon Papers: The Defense Department History of United States Decisionmaking on Vietnam.* Vols. 1, 2, 3, 4. Boston: Beacon Press, 1971.

Griffith, Elisabeth. *In Her Own Right: The Life of Elizabeth Cady Stanton.* New York: Oxford University Press, 1984.

Gustafson, James M. *Ethics from a Theocentric Perspective.* Chicago: University of Chicago Press, 1981.

Haddox, M. Bruce. "Self, Society, and Stories: Reflections on Thinking." Unpublished manuscript, 1978.

Hardesty, Nancy. *Women Called to Witness.* Nashville: Abingdon Press, 1984.

Harding, Vincent. "Out of the Cauldron of Struggle." *Soundings* 61, no. 3 (Fall 1978), pp. 339–53.

_____ . *There Is a River.* New York: Harcourt Brace Jovanovich, 1981.

Harrison, Beverly Wildung. *Making the Connections.* Boston: Beacon Press, 1985.

_____ . *Our Right to Choose.* Boston: Beacon Press, 1983.

Hauerwas, Stanley. *A Community of Character.* Notre Dame, Ind.: Notre Dame Press, 1981.

_____ . *The Peaceable Kingdom.* Notre Dame, Ind.: Notre Dame Press, 1983.

_____ . *Vision and Virtue.* Notre Dame, Ind.: Fides, 1974.

_____ , et al. *Truthfulness and Tragedy.* Notre Dame, Ind.: Notre Dame Press, 1977.

Herberg, Will. *Protestant, Catholic, Jew.* Garden City, N.Y.: Doubleday & Co., 1960.

Hillman, James. "The Fiction of Case History: A Round." In James B. Wiggins, ed., *Religion as Story.*

_____. *Re-Visioning Psychology.* New York: Harper & Row, 1975.

Hofstadter, Richard. *Social Darwinism in American Thought.* Boston: Beacon Press, 1955.

_____, ed. *The Progressive Movement.* Englewood Cliffs, N.J.: Prentice-Hall, 1963.

Homans, Peter. *Jung in Context.* Chicago: University of Chicago Press, 1979.

Jacques-Garvey, Amy, ed. *Philosophy and Opinions of Marcus Garvey.* New York: Arno Press, 1968.

James, Janet Wilson, ed. *Women in American Religion.* Philadelphia: University of Pennsylvania Press, 1980.

Johnson, Lyndon B. *The Vantage Point.* New York: Holt, Rinehart & Winston, 1971.

Jung, C. G. *Memories, Dreams, Reflections.* New York: Vintage Books, 1965.

Kelsey, George D. *Racism and the Christian Understanding of Man.* New York: Charles Scribner's Sons, 1965.

Kennedy, David M. *Over Here.* New York: Oxford University Press, 1980.

Kennedy, Gail. *Democracy and the Gospel of Wealth.* Boston: D. C. Heath & Co., 1949.

Kennedy, John F. "Inaugural Address." In *The Annals of America,* vol. 18. Chicago: Encyclopedia Britannica, 1974.

Kermode, Frank. *The Genesis of Secrecy.* Cambridge, Mass.: Harvard University Press, 1979.

_____. *The Sense of an Ending.* London: Oxford University Press, 1966.

King, Martin Luther, Jr. *Stride Toward Freedom.* New York: Harper & Row, 1958.

_____. *Where Do We Go from Here: Chaos or Community?* New York: Harper & Row, 1967.

Lasch, Christopher. *The Culture of Narcissism.* New York: W. W. Norton & Co., 1979.

Lears, T. J. Jackson. *No Place of Grace.* New York: Pantheon Books, 1981.

Lerner, Gerda. *The Grimké Sisters from South Carolina.* Boston: Houghton Mifflin Co., 1967.

Levy, Jacques E. *Cesar Chavez: Autobiography of La Causa.* New York: W. W. Norton & Co., 1966.

Lincoln, Abraham. "The Second Inaugural Address." In *The Annals of America,* vols. 9 and 20. Chicago: Encyclopedia Britannica, 1974.

Long, Edward LeRoy. *War and Conscience in America.* Philadelphia: Westminster Press, 1968.

Maccoby, Michael. *The Gamesman.* New York: Simon & Schuster, 1976.

MacHaffie, Barbara J. *Her Story.* Philadelphia: Fortress Press, 1986.

MacIntyre, Alasdair. *After Virtue.* Notre Dame, Ind.: Notre Dame Press, 1981.

Maclear, J. F. "The Republic and the Millennium." In E. A. Smith, *The Religion of the Republic.* Philadelphia: Fortress Press, 1971.

Malcolm X. *The Autobiography of Malcolm X.* New York: Grove Press, 1964.

Marty, Martin E. *Modern American Religion.* Chicago: University of Chicago Press, 1986.

———. *Pilgrims in Their Own Land.* New York: Penguin Books, 1984.

Marx, Leo. *The Machine in the Garden.* New York: Oxford University Press, 1964.

Mather, Cotton. *Bonifacius: An Essay to Do Good.* Gainesville, Fla.: Scholars' Facsimiles & Reprints, 1967.

May, Henry F. *The End of American Innocence.* New York: Alfred A. Knopf, 1959.

———. *The Enlightenment in America.* New York: Oxford University Press, 1976.

———. *Ideas, Faiths, and Feelings.* New York: Oxford University Press, 1983.

McCarthy, Eugene J. *The Year of the People.* Garden City, N.Y.: Doubleday & Co., 1969.

McClendon, James W., Jr. *Biography as Theology.* Nashville: Abingdon Press, 1974.

———, and James M. Smith. *Understanding Religious Convictions.* Notre Dame, Ind.: Notre Dame Press, 1975.

McClendon, James W., Jr., and Axel D. Steuer, eds., *Is God God?* Nashville: Abingdon Press, 1981.

McFague, Sallie. *Metaphorical Theology.* Philadelphia: Fortress Press, 1982.

McGuffey, William Holmes. *McGuffey's Fifth Eclectic Reader.* Cincinnati: American Book Co., 1879.

McLoughlin, William G. *Revivals, Awakenings and Reform.* Chicago: University of Chicago Press, 1978.

Mead, Sidney. *The Lively Experiment.* New York: Harper & Row, 1963.

_____. *The Nation with the Soul of a Church.* New York: Harper & Row, 1975.

Melville, Herman. *White Jacket.* Quoted in Ernest L. Tuveson, *Redeemer Nation.*

Merk, Frederick. *Manifest Destiny and Mission in American History.* New York: Alfred A. Knopf, 1963.

Meyer, Donald. *The Positive Thinkers.* New York: Pantheon Books, 1980.

Miller, Arthur. *Death of a Salesman.* New York: Viking Press, 1949.

Miller, Perry. *Errand Into the Wilderness,* New York: Harper & Row, 1956.

_____, ed. *The American Puritans.* Garden City, N.Y.: Doubleday & Co., Anchor Books, 1956.

Miller, William D. *Dorothy Day: A Biography.* San Francisco: Harper & Row, 1982.

Millett, Kate. *Sexual Politics.* New York: Avon Books, 1969.

Morgan, Edmund S. *The Puritan Dilemma.* Boston: Little, Brown & Co., 1958.

_____. *Roger Williams.* New York: Harcourt, Brace & World, 1967.

Morison, Samuel Eliot. *The Oxford History of the American People.* New York: Oxford University Press, 1965.

National Conference of Catholic Bishops. *The Challenge of Peace.* Washington, D. C.: United States Catholic Conference, 1983.

Newfield, Jack. *Robert Kennedy: A Memoir.* New York: E. P. Dutton & Co., 1969.

Niebuhr, H. Richard. *The Kingdom of God in America.* New York: Harper & Row, 1937.

_____. *Radical Monotheism and Western Culture.* New York: Harper & Row, 1960.

_____. *The Responsible Self.* New York: Harper & Row, 1963.

Niebuhr, Reinhold. *The Irony of American History.* New York: Charles Scribner's Sons, 1952.

_____. *Moral Man and Immoral Society.* New York: Charles Scribner's Sons, 1932.

_____. *A Nation So Conceived.* New York: Charles Scribner's Sons, 1963.

Nye, Russel B. *This Almost Chosen People.* East Lansing, Mich.: Michigan State University Press, 1966.

Oates, Stephen B. *Let the Trumpet Sound: The Life of Martin Luther King, Jr.* New York: Harper & Row, 1982.

Ogletree, Thomas. *The Use of the Bible in Christian Ethics.* Philadelphia: Fortress Press, 1983.

O'Neill, Nena, and George O'Neill. *Open Marriage.* New York: Avon Books, 1972.

O'Neill, William L. *Everyone Was Brave.* Chicago: Quadrangle Books, 1969.

Paris, Peter J. *The Social Teaching of the Black Churches.* Philadelphia: Fortress Press, 1985.

Peale, Norman Vincent. *The Power of Positive Thinking.* New York: Ballantine Books, 1952.

Polanyi, Michael. *Personal Knowledge.* Chicago: University of Chicago Press, 1958.

Porterfield, Amanda. *Feminine Spirituality in America: From Sarah Edwards to Martha Graham.* Philadelphia: Temple University Press, 1980.

Raskin, Marcus G., and Bernard B. Fall, eds. *The Viet-Nam Reader.* New York: Vintage Books, 1967.

Richey, Russell E., and Donald G. Jones. *American Civil Religion.* New York: Harper & Row, 1974.

Rieff, Philip. *Freud: The Mind of the Moralist.* Garden City, N.Y.: Doubleday & Co., Anchor Books, 1961.

———. *The Triumph of the Therapeutic.* New York: Harper & Row, 1968.

Riesman, David. *The Lonely Crowd.* New Haven, Conn.: Yale University Press, 1961.

Rothman, Sheila M. *Woman's Proper Place.* New York: Basic Books, 1978.

Ruether, Rosemary Radford. *New Woman—New Earth: Sexist Ideologies and Human Liberation.* New York: Seabury Press, 1975.

———. *Sexism and God-Talk: Toward a Feminist Theology.* Boston: Beacon Press, 1983.

———, and Rosemary Skinner Keller, eds. *Women and Religion in America.* Vols. 1, 2. San Francisco: Harper & Row, 1981, 1983.

Ryan, Mary P. *Womanhood in America.* New York: Franklin Watts, 1979.

Sanford, Charles L. *Benjamin Franklin and the American Character.* Boston: D. C. Heath & Co., 1955.

Schickel, Richard. *His Picture in the Papers.* New York: Charterhouse Books, 1973.

Schlesinger, Arthur M., Jr. *The Cycles of American History.* Boston: Houghton Mifflin Co., 1986.

_____. *Robert Kennedy and His Times.* Boston: Houghton Mifflin Co., 1965.

_____. *A Thousand Days: John F. Kennedy in the White House.* Boston: Houghton Mifflin Co., 1965.

Scholes, Robert, and Robert Kellogg. *The Nature of Narrative.* New York: Oxford University Press, 1966.

Schuller, Robert H. *Self-Esteem.* Waco, Tex.: Word Books, 1982.

_____. *Tough Times Never Last, but Tough People Do!* New York: Thomas Nelson, 1983.

Sewell, Elizabeth. *The Human Metaphor.* Notre Dame, Ind.: Notre Dame Press, 1964.

Smith, Henry N. *Virgin Land.* Cambridge, Mass., Harvard University Press, 1950.

Steel, Ronald. *Pax Americana.* New York: Viking Press, 1967.

Steuer, Axel D., and George Stroup. *The Promise of Narrative Theology.* Atlanta: John Knox Press, 1981.

Stiles, Ezra. "The United States Elevated to Glory and Honor." In Conrad Cherry, ed., *God's New Israel.*

Strong, Josiah. *Our Country.* Cambridge, Mass.: Belknap Press, 1963.

Susman, Warren. *Culture as History.* New York: Pantheon Books, 1984.

_____. " 'Personality' and the Making of Twentieth-Century Culture." In John Higham and Paul Conkin, *New Directions in American Intellectual History.* Baltimore: Johns Hopkins University Press, 1979.

Talbert, Charles H. *Reading Luke.* New York: Crossroad Publishing Co., 1982.

Trachtenberg, Alan. *The Incorporation of America.* New York: Hill & Wang, 1982.

Tuveson, Ernest L. *Redeemer Nation.* Chicago: University of Chicago Press, 1968.

Tyler, Alice. *Freedom's Ferment.* New York: Harper & Row, 1944.

United Methodist Council of Bishops. *In Defense of Creation: The Nuclear Crisis and a Just Peace.* Nashville: Graded Press, 1986.

Van Alstyne, R. W. *The Rising American Empire.* London: Oxford University Press, 1960.

Van Doren, Carl. *Benjamin Franklin.* New York: Viking Press, 1953.

Veroff, Joseph. *The Inner American.* New York: Basic Books, 1981.

Von Rad, Gerhard. *Old Testament Theology.* vol. 1, 2. Edinburgh: Oliver & Boyd, 1962.

Wayland, Francis. Quoted in J. F. Maclear, "The Republic and the Millennium," in E. A. Smith, *The Religion of the Republic.* Philadelphia: Fortress Press, 1971.

Wall, Joseph F. *Andrew Carnegie.* New York: Oxford University Press, 1970.

Weber, Max. *The Protestant Ethic and the Spirit of Capitalism.* New York: Charles Scribner's Sons, 1958.

Weidman, Judith L. *Christian Feminism.* San Francisco: Harper & Row, 1984.

Weiss, Richard. *The American Myth of Success.* New York: Basic Books, 1969.

Wells, Ronald A., ed. *The Wars of America.* Grand Rapids: Wm. B. Eerdmans Publishing Co., 1981.

West, Cornel. *Prophesy Deliverance!* Philadelphia: Westminster Press, 1982.

Wicker, Brian. *The Story-Shaped World.* Notre Dame, Ind.: Notre Dame Press, 1975.

Wiggins, James B., ed. *Religion as Story.* New York: Harper & Row, 1975.

Williams, Selma R. *Divine Rebel: The Life of Anne Marbury Hutchinson.* New York: Holt, Rinehart & Winston, 1981.

Wilmore, Gayraud S. *Black Religion and Black Radicalism.* 2nd ed. Maryknoll, N.Y.: Orbis Books, 1985.

————, and James H. Cone. *Black Theology: A Documentary History, 1966–1979.* Maryknoll, N.Y.: Orbis Books, 1979.

Winslow, Ola E. *Jonathan Edwards.* New York: Collier Books, 1961.

Wyllie, Irvin G. *The Self-made Man in America.* New York: Free Press, 1954.

Yankelovich, Daniel. *New Rules.* New York: Bantam Books, 1982.

Yeager, Diane. "The Web of Relationship: Feminists and Christians." In *Soundings* 71, no. 4 (Winter, 1988).

Yezierska, Anzia. *Bread Givers.* New York: Persea Books, 1975.

Yoder, John Howard. *The Politics of Jesus.* Grand Rapids: Wm. B. Eerdmans Publishing Co., 1972.

Index